CONTENTS

By Definition...7

Letters from Hendrick Motorsports 9

Long and Winding Road 11

First Strike: 2006...13

Second That Emotion: 2007 33

Photo Gallery 67

Triple Crown: 2008...75

Making History: 2009 101

JJ Wins by Year...126

BY DEFINITION
Jimmie Johnson Establishes a Dynasty

In sports, the word "dynasty" is tossed around too loosely. The New England Patriots won four Super Bowl titles in six years and were immediately credited with establishing a dynasty. Does that qualify?

Certainly, the Boston Celtics eight-year run as NBA champions from 1959–66 makes the cut and hockey's Montreal Canadiens five consecutive Stanley Cups from 1956–60 qualifies. Most impressive might be the stranglehold the UCLA Bruins maintained on NCAA basketball titles from 1964–73.

Dynasties have to be special.

From 2006–09, Jimmie Johnson did something very special. He became the only driver to win four consecutive NASCAR Cup championships in the sport's storied history. The dominant run broke a record held by Cale Yarbrough and left Johnson standing above his competition in a way that legends such as Richard Petty and Dale Earnhardt never realized.

By no means a specialist or one-trick pony, Johnson exhibited his mastery on short tracks, road courses, intermediate ovals, and superspeedways.

He even conquered mighty Indianapolis Motor Speedway three times. And he did all of this in two completely different rides: NASCAR's old car and the "car of tomorrow."

With award-winning stories and photography, two publications—NASCAR Scene and NASCAR Illustrated—took fans along for Johnson's incredible run. For this special commemorative book, we collected the original race coverage of Johnson's 29 wins from Scene and Illustrated and uncovered many never-before-published photographs, which we are excited to share with you.

Johnson's victories are all here, including two remarkable wins—one, the Daytona 500—during a six-race suspension of crew chief, Chad Knaus, in 2006 and the late-race bump of Denny Hamlin to seal a victory at Martinsville in March 2009.

During his historic run, Johnson never lost sight of the importance of teamwork at Hendrick Motorsports and his partnership with all members of Team Lowe's Racing.

—**Michael J. Fresina, Publisher**
NASCAR Illustrated, NASCAR Scene, SceneDaily.com

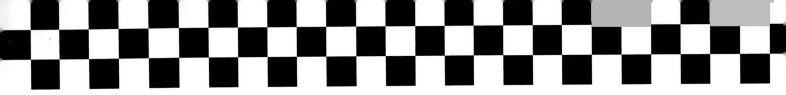

To Our Lowe's Teammates,

On behalf of your more than 500 teammates at Hendrick Motorsports, thank you for another unbelievable race season! Jimmie Johnson, Chad Knaus and your 48 team made history in 2009 by winning their fourth consecutive NASCAR Sprint Cup championship.

As I reflect upon this accomplishment, I am humbled by the great success we have achieved together with Lowe's as our partner. We thank you for your supports and remain so proud to represent you each and every week, both on and off of the racetrack.

We look forward to taking another historical ride with you next year and beyond.

Sincerely,

Rick Hendrick

Rick Hendrick

To My Friends At Lowe's,

Congratulations on another winning season for Lowe's and the 48 team. This year has been amazing and I couldn't have accomplished this fourth straight championship without your support and encouragement each week as we represent Lowe's on the track.

I am humbled and proud to be chosen to represent Lowe's and each of the employee/owners that make it possible for me to do what I love each week. I am still trying to take in all the we have accomplished together this year and I am sure as time goes on, it will all sink in.

Thank you for all your partnership and support throughout all of the years together. I am looking forward to another great year in 2010 and can't wait to see you all in Daytona.

Best Racing Wishes,

Jimmie Johnson

Jimmie Johnson
4-Time Sprint Cup Champion

To Our Lowe's Teammates,

First and foremost, congratulations to each and every one of you on this amazing 2009 season. Thank you all for supporting us through these championships over the past four years as we have made NASCAR history together.

Each week throughout the season, the No. 48 team races for all the employee associates at Lowe's that make it possible for us to do what we love—race. When we win, you win. We've shared so much success throughout the partnership with Hendrick Motorsports, and we're excited to share much, much more in the future.

We are very proud to represent Lowe's both on our race cars and in our shop. We couldn't do it without you.

See you in the winner's circle,

Chad Knaus

Chad Knaus
Crew Chief of the No. 48 Lowe's Chevrolet

LONG AND WINDING ROAD

Jimmie Johnson Followed an Unusual Path to NASCAR Championship

Pressure. Nerves. Butterflies. All would seem to be foreign terms to four-time Sprint Cup champion Jimmie Johnson.

During one of the most remarkable runs in NASCAR history, Johnson has shown few signs of feeling the jitters that most athletes endure during big-game situations, or with a championship on the line.

But that wasn't always the case.

As he sat on pit road at Lowe's Motor Speedway on Oct. 7, 2001, Johnson was feeling the heat.

He was attempting to qualify for his first Sprint Cup race for vaunted Hendrick Motorsports.

This was his big chance. Johnson had landed a golden opportunity as the driver for a brand-new team for the most successful organization in NASCAR. He didn't want to blow it or embarrass the organization by failing to qualify in his very first attempt.

"At that point, I was just worried about making the event," Johnson said. "I really didn't have a lot of pressure from anyone. Those three races were a chance for me to get my feet wet. I just remember the pressure of qualifying, getting in the show."

Johnson made the show that day, but it was an inauspicious debut. He started 15th but crashed and finished 39th.

He finished 25th and 29th in the final two races of the season, offering few hints that he

would be a force with his new team.

There was little evidence, in fact, that Johnson would become a star.

The son of a blue-collar family from El Cajon, Calif., Johnson began his career racing motorcycles at age 5. He rose through the ranks, eventually switching to off-road racing, where he won six championships.

His transition to stock cars, however, was not exactly smooth.

Johnson was rookie of the year in the American Speed Association in 1998 before making the leap to NASCAR's Busch Series.

the shoulder and ask me for that advice."

Gordon was so impressed with Johnson that he recommended him to team owner Rick Hendrick, who was in the process of starting a fourth Sprint Cup team.

Gordon soon became co-owner of Johnson's No. 48 team and Johnson's unofficial mentor.

"Somebody was going to pick him up, and I'm just really thankful that the opportunity presented itself to us," Gordon said.

After getting his feet wet with those three races in 2001, Johnson took the series by storm as a rookie in 2002. He scored six top-10 finishes in his first nine races, and then won the 10th race of the season at California Speedway, his home track.

His early season success launched what turned out as a breakout season for the young driver. Johnson won two more races (both at Dover) and finished fifth in points – a sign of things to come.

"I knew deep down inside that I needed to win a race [my rookie year]," Johnson says. "I needed to make my mark in that 48 car, especially with Jeff coming off a championship year."

And make his mark he did, even before his first championship season in 2006.

Over the next three years, Johnson won 15 races, including a career-high eight in 2004, and finished second in points twice. He finished second to Matt Kenseth in 2003 and missed winning the inaugural Chase by just eight points in 2004. He trailed champion Tony Stewart in 2005 before crashing in the final race and slumping to fifth in points.

Four top-five points finishes and 18 victories in his first four seasons served notice that Johnson was indeed on the verge of greatness.

It has all come as a pleasant surprise for the humble champion.

"I have so much to be thankful for," Johnson said.

—Jeff Owens

In two full seasons of Busch competition, he had only marginal success, winning just one race and scoring only four top-five finishes in 64 starts for Herzog Motorsports.

That he even landed a lucrative ride with Hendrick was a bit of a surprise. It was due more to his courage and determination than his success on the track.

Though he was struggling in the Busch Series, Johnson approached four-time Cup champion Jeff Gordon, seeking advice about his next career move. It was that move that opened the door at Hendrick.

"I give Jimmie a lot of the credit," Gordon said. "He came to me and just asked me some opinions about car owners and teams and what his next move should be. I was really kind of blown away for him to look up to me in that way, to come tap me on

FIGHTING BACK

Jimmie Johnson Nabs Daytona 500 Win without Crew Chief

Daytona 500 • NASCAR NEXTEL CUP Race No. 1
Feb. 19, 2006 • Daytona Beach, Fla. • Daytona International Speedway • 203 Laps

Controversy swirled around Jimmie Johnson throughout Speedweeks after crew chief Chad Knaus was ejected from the track for a rules infraction.

Knaus had been collared for an illegal device that altered the aerodynamics of Johnson's Chevrolet during qualifying and Johnson was left to weather a storm of controversy.

With Knaus at home, team engineer Darian Grubb, who sits atop the pit box next to Knaus during races, slid over a spot and served as Johnson's crew chief.

And despite all the distractions, Johnson went on to claim his first Daytona 500 victory — the sixth for Hendrick Motorsports.

Following his win, Johnson was defiant: "I'm dedicating this to the haters of the 48 team. We won, and we're in victory lane for the Daytona 500."

Johnson's comments didn't exactly clear the air. In fact, some questioned the validity of Johnson's Daytona 500 victory.

Johnson dismissed all the accusations.

"I think it's the complete opposite," he said. "There's a black mark next to qualifying. But the race, with the circumstances we've been through, and the situation that we're in, we overcame everybody against us. I mean, every single media person, every single crew member."

With 19 wins going into the 500, Johnson had learned that survival was the first order of business at restrictor-plate tracks. This time, he stayed out of the big fights.

Lingering among the top 10, Johnson knew the best time to strike was in the closing laps. He

scooted around teammate Brain Vickers to lead lap 187, survived a green-white-checkered finish and snared the victory.

"Today was one of the hardest races for me mentally because the racer in me wanted to push and wanted to be aggressive out there," Johnson said. "There were so many times I just told myself to stop."

Grubb, who will lead the team for three more events after NASCAR suspended Knaus until March 22, was on the brink of tears following the win. Maintaining his composure, he soaked it all in and, like a good soldier, heaped praise upon Knaus.

"I just want to thank Chad for building this team the way he has," Grubb said. "This job is very hard. I don't want to kid anybody about that. Chad has always done a great job, but he has trained me well. I've worked with him for three years straight. I think I've learned everything I've ever learned from him.

"I know it had to have killed him to be home, but we owe it all to him. He has really supported us in everything we have done. He let us run our own show. We made all the changes we wanted to make."

—Ben White

WEATHER OR NOT

Johnson Overcomes Cold Conditions

UAW-DaimlerChrysler 400 • NASCAR Nextel Cup Race No. 3
March 12, 2006 • Las Vegas, Nev. • Las Vegas Motor Speedway • 270 Laps

In spite of unusually cool weather, Jimmie Johnson continued his torrid start in Las Vegas. Putting the finishing touches on a historic first-second-first start to the 2006 season, Johnson laid in wait throughout the race, saving his best for the very last. Johnson's last-second surge past Matt Kenseth sealed the win and extended his points lead in the young season.

Despite the exciting ending, most of the race followed the new template for mile-and-a-half tracks. That is, it looked like another Roush sweep. Kenseth and Mark Martin, both former winners at the Las Vegas track, led a total of 203 laps.

However, Johnson and interim crew chief Darian Grubb, managed to negate the difficult conditions to snare the win. After Chad Knaus' suspension in Daytona, Grubb's storybook tenure is the stuff of legend.

He and Johnson fought through the unseasonable cold that threw most teams for a loop. Prepared for hot conditions and slippery pavement, crews scrambled to get their cars in shape for the 40-degree temperatures.

"It was tough. I didn't want to make a mistake and crash the car trying to get extra speed out of it," Johnson said. "There were times today where

we were a little too tight and some cars were faster than us and I just pulled down and let them go. I really tried to focus on my car for three-quarters of the race and make sure I had the best driving race car I could."

The cold made most cars tight, especially in the center of the corners, and many teams overcompensated, loosening their cars too much.

Third-place finisher Kyle Busch may have been able to give Kenseth and Johnson a better race had his Chevrolet not danced all over the track in the closing laps.

"I was going to come over the radio and ask if the weather had changed because I started getting a little looser," Busch said. "We kept loosening up my car all day and finally it got so loose that I was barely hanging on. We had to come back off those changes in the last pit stop. But we didn't come back off enough because I was still too loose at the end."

Chassis setups also pushed tires up to, and in some cases, past the breaking point. Ryan Newman and Reed Sorenson crashed due to blown right front tires and both felt that chassis setups played into the equation.

"We had cords the first run," Newman said. "We freed the car way up, and we were looser the second run. The car got tighter and tighter each lap. Goodyear's got some work to do. I'm stuck. I'm running as hard as I can to try to get my lap back. It's just unfortunate. I thought we had a better race car than that."

This was also the last race on the familiar, wide Las Vegas track. To make racing more competitive, major track remodeling will put more banking in the turns and reconfigure pit road. When NASCAR returns in March 2007, the drivers will face an entirely new surface.

—Ben White

EVERY MAN FOR HIMSELF

No Honor Among Teammates with Five to Go

Aaron's 499 • NASCAR Nextel Cup Race No. 9
May 1, 2006 • Talladega, Ala. • Talladega Superspeedway • 188 Laps

Once the green flag finally waved over the rain-delayed Aaron's 499 at Talladega Superspeedway, there was no doubt which racing organization brought the most horsepower to the show.

Hendrick Motorsports, featuring drivers Jeff Gordon, Jimmie Johnson, Brian Vickers and Kyle Busch (who fell from contention following a lap-9 accident), unloaded with fast cars as Gordon, Johnson

and Vickers constantly ran at or near the front of Talladega's tight packs.

In restrictor-plate racing, it is essential to have friends on the track willing to help work the draft. And the Hendrick drivers repeatedly worked together to stay up front.

The partnerships ended, however, in the closing laps as each of the three drivers gunned for the win.

A victory would have moved Gordon up the point standings — as well as sent a clear message to his competitors that the four-time champ can still will his team to a win.

Johnson, meanwhile, wanted to prove he could take the checkered flag on a superspeedway without controversy.

And Vickers simply wanted to win, something he has not yet done in 86 Nextel Cup starts.

Gordon moved out front for the first time on lap 8 after starting 14th and led a race-high 62 laps — 39 more than the next closest driver, polesitter Elliott Sadler. However, Gordon's hopes of winning a fifth time at the 2.66-mile track faded as he slipped to 15th in a wild last-lap shuffle.

And as Vickers closed in on the checkered flag,

Johnson snatched the lead heading into Turn 1 on the final lap.

"We all know it's just about when things cycle out and if you time it to lead the last lap," Johnson said. "I said to my crew guys on the cool-down lap, 'That kid [Vickers] did an awesome job today and deserves to win a lot of these races.' I didn't regret the move, but I feel for him. And he's going to have plenty of wins in the near future."

Vickers, who led four times for seven laps, didn't blame Johnson.

"When it comes down to the last lap, I can't expect anything out of those guys," Vickers said. "If they go with me, great, I'll go give them a hug afterwards. But if they don't, I'm not going to hold it against them."

Teammates or not, Gordon understands the track gets very lonely with the checkered flag in sight.

"[My teammates] have got to do what they've got to do," Gordon said. "I've always done it that way. I've always preached to them that way. They did exactly what I would have done.

"Once you get inside five to go, you've got to go."

—Ben White

FEELING THE DRAFT

After his aggressive driving drew criticism at last spring's Talladega Superspeedway race, Jimmie Johnson took a wait-and-see approach for the majority of the rain-delayed Aaron's 499. Leading only three of 188 laps, Johnson held off Hendrick Motorsports teammates Jeff Gordon and Brian Vickers and a pack of determined rivals en route to his third win of the season.

Caution flags slowed the event eight times for 34 laps, including two multicar accidents on laps 9 and 174 involving 19 drivers. The white-knuckle restrictor-plate event excited fans with 56 lead changes among 22 drivers and four- and five-wide racing.

"I probably was hung out more times than I wanted to be.... But I didn't want to be aggressive," Johnson said. "I didn't want to block anyone. If somebody got position on me before the spotter said it, I just let it go and then fought my way back through there."

BRICK BY BRICK
Workmanlike Effort Nets Johnson Indy Win

Allstate 400 at The Brickyard • NASCAR Nextel Cup Race No. 21
Aug. 6, 2006 • Indianapolis, Ind. • Indianapolis Motor Speedway • 160 Laps

Once again, Jimmie Johnson hit a stretch of bad luck at Indy. But this time, Johnson and the No. 48 crew overcame their poor fortune.

The Lowe's team fought through dead radio batteries, tire problems and even a pit road fire to claim the win in the Allstate 400 at the Brickyard.

The victory offered tantalizing evidence that the team's championship luck may be changing.

After bad runs at Indy derailed Johnson's championship campaigns over the past two seasons, the win seemed to lift a great weight from his shoulders.

"I'm speechless right now. I can't thank this race team for all that they've done," Johnson said. "I just can't believe we overcame all the things we have at this race track and the challenges we had today and won."

A cut left front tire on lap 40 of the 160-lap event briefly caused panic among his team, but a competition caution by NASCAR the next lap to check tire wear was the break they needed to stay in contention.

"The issue we had with the tire, I have to admit, it really deflated me inside the car," Johnson said. "I thought, 'Man, it's going to be impossible to pass here.' The tire started coming apart when I was trying

to get back to pit road. I thought it destroyed the fender and really took us out of contention."

Johnson spent the day proving why he's atop the Nextel Cup point standings. After Jeff Burton started from the pole position and set the pace by leading a race-high 87 laps, Kevin Harvick and Matt Kenseth got out front. But Johnson had the car to beat.

He carefully moved through the field, gaining the top spot for the first time on lap 117. He took it again on lap 128 and held it for good once he wrested it from Kyle Busch on lap 151.

Second-place finisher Kenseth simply had

NOT THIS TIME

Jimmie Johnson overcame a flat left front tire early in the race and a late caution period to win the Allstate 400 at Indianapolis Motor Speedway.

Johnson led the 160-lap event three times for 33 laps en route to his fourth victory of the season and first at the Brickyard.

After building a comfortable lead, a caution for debris on lap 143 leveled the field and made Johnson work for the win. While Johnson and Matt Kenseth and many others pitted for four tires and fuel, Kyle Busch, Kevin Harvick and Dale Earnhardt Jr. stayed out and took the green flag with Busch leading.

Restarting eighth, Johnson tracked them down one by one and got around Busch for the lead, holding it over the final 10 laps.

Kenseth took second, with Harvick sneaking into third, Clint Bowyer in fourth and Mark Martin in fifth.

After dismal finishes at Indianapolis two years in a row, Johnson was almost dumbstruck after he took the flag.

"I never thought I'd ever win at this race track," he said. "We've had such a drought at this race track, and now we've got a victory."

nothing for Johnson at the end.

"He was real strong," Kenseth said. "We were kind of gauging and adjusting against the 29 [Harvick] and the 31 [Burton] ... and I thought if we were in front of them, we had it good enough to maybe beat them guys, but then the 48 kind of came out of nowhere. He was just flying."

Several drivers recorded strong finishes by not pitting during the final caution on lap 143. Dale Earnhardt Jr., Kyle Busch, Ryan Newman and Joe Nemechek gambled by staying out and

their wager paid off.

Earnhardt, for one, logged a sixth-place finish, putting him back in the top 10 in the point standings after back-to-back last-place finishes at Loudon and Pocono.

"When we say our prayers, we will thank the Lord for this one because we really got lucky," Earnhardt said. "We can't make the Chase with 30th-place race cars."

Some drivers, however, did not have such good fortune. While Junior rallied, Kasey Kahne's Chase hopes took a shot. On the last lap, Kahne got loose as he battled Tony Stewart and hit the wall. The crash cost him a possible top-10 finish and left in 36th. It also dropped him from fourth to 11th in the Chase standings.

"I was trying to get in a battle with all those guys for position," Kahne said. "I had to block [Carl] Edwards and come back to [Tony] Stewart. ... Stewart got right down on me, I got loose and then I just tried staying off Tony I guess and ran into the wall."

—Ben White

SHORT TRACK SHUFFLE

Chase Back on After Martinsville

Subway 500 • NASCAR Nextel Cup Race No. 32
Oct. 22, 2006 • Martinsville, Va. • Martinsville Speedway • 500 Laps

Jimmie Johnson breathed new life into his championship aspirations with a win in the Subway 500 at Martinsville Speedway. The win moved Johnson from seventh to third in the standings — 41 points behind new championship frontrunner Matt Kenseth.

Johnson had a stout car, but pit strategy turned out to be the deciding factor.

Crew chief Chad Knaus brought his driver to pit road for a four-tire stop on lap 244 of 500. While just three cars followed him, the strategy paid off as Johnson took the lead during the next caution when everyone else pitted.

Johnson edged out rookie Denny Hamlin for the win, but Hamlin made the Hendrick driver earn the victory.

Hamlin tapped Johnson's rear bumper twice off Turn 2 late in the race, trying to get alongside him. He did, but Johnson nearly drove Hamlin into the infield as the two raced to Turn 3.

"I had a better car for about three or four laps after a restart," Hamlin said. "He was better after that. It was my only shot to get around him."

They banged again, but Johnson's car only got stronger, and he sped away.

"I knew I was going to get the bumper at some

point," Johnson said. "That's just the way it is. He got to me, he got on me. Once he got beside me, I expressed my displeasure and pinched him down to the inside wall. Once I got position back, he didn't take any more shots at me.

"He went right to the line. He didn't cross it. It was all good."

Of course, Johnson can say that, since he won the race. But Hamlin wasn't going to wreck Johnson, either.

"I wasn't going to get under him cleanly," Hamlin said. "There was no way possible. I owe it to my team to try the best I can to win a race, and I did get into him. Yeah, it was on purpose, but I didn't want to wreck him. I didn't want to pass him and clear him that way.

"I just wanted to get beside him that way, and we were able to do that. He proved he had a better car on the outside, and the best car won. Probably the best driver, too."

With Johnson coming on strong late in the season, will he have enough to challenge for the championship?

"We're just showing up and racing at this point," Johnson said. "Where it finishes up, it finishes up. We've been in the hunt for the championship every year this team's been around. Sooner or later, we're going to get one."

Bobby Labonte had his best run of the season and finished third. Tony Stewart was fourth and Jeff Gordon finished fifth.

Jeff Burton fell from first to fifth in the standings after a poor finish. He lost a lap after NASCAR made his No. 31 Richard Childress Racing team make cosmetic repairs to a slightly damaged hood.

Then, Burton's day continued to sour when he reported an engine problem. After discussions between car owner Richard Childress and crew chief Scott Miller, Burton went behind the wall. He never came back, finishing 42nd.

"I'm pretty disappointed, but at the same time, everybody has had trouble," Burton said. "It was our turn today. I still feel like this team is very capable of winning the championship. I feel like this team will fight. We are a very resilient group. We won't lay down."

Burton's engine failure gave everyone in the Chase a chance to gain ground. With Burton sliding to third, Matt Kenseth assumed the lead — but every driver in the top five stayed within 48 points of the lead. His good fortune notwithstanding, Kenseth was by no means happy after the race.

"You know, we haven't run good in this Chase," Kenseth said. "We ran good at Dover, we ran good at Talladega, and other than that, we haven't looked like a championship team. It's great to be the leader, but we've got to start running good."

—**Ben White**

FINALLY, A CHAMPION

Jimmie Johnson Wins the Chase to Claim Elusive Nextel Cup Championship

This time, despite the last-lap smoke at Talladega, despite a sour Chase opener, Jimmie Johnson would not be denied. He had been close enough to the Nextel Cup to taste it; indeed, he could see the emblem of NASCAR excellence almost any time he wanted because five Cup trophies are housed at Hendrick Motorsports' suburban Charlotte shop.

This time, after being second twice and fifth twice in his short Cup career, Johnson sealed the deal. Three hundred miles south of Daytona Beach, where his quest began with a Daytona 500 victory in February, Johnson finished a safe ninth in the Ford 400 to win the 2006 championship by 56 points over second-place Matt Kenseth. Kenseth, who was sixth in the race, entered the day 63 points behind Johnson and needed a mediocre-to-poor performance by Johnson to have a realistic shot at winning the championship.

This time, on this day, in this place, that didn't happen. Johnson led only two laps but was consistently in the top 15 and in sight of the lead pack. His team's only minor miscue was a loose lug nut on a pit stop, and that was corrected before Johnson could bolt from his pit, thanks to the eagle eye of crew chief Chad Knaus. Debris from an early race crash by Kurt Busch knocked a hole in the valance of Johnson's car, but the incident didn't cause a significant problem.

Three hours later, as Greg Biffle took the checkered flag, Johnson had his first title after driving so close to the top in the four previous seasons.

"People thought and expected a lot out of us as a race team from the beginning," Johnson said. "We never felt a burden [of expectation]. Don't get me wrong. We didn't want to miss an opportunity when we were in the position to become a champion.

We've just been happy to win races and have the season we had."

Johnson, 31, won the season-opening Daytona 500 and led the point standings after 22 of the first 26 races, giving him a head of steam going into the 10-race Chase For The Nextel Cup. He entered the Chase second to Kenseth.

In the first Chase race, at New Hampshire, Johnson's car dropped a cylinder early and he was swept into a crash. Result? 39th place. A week later at Dover, Johnson was 13th, followed by a 14th at Kansas. Then came Talladega and one of the season's most dramatic moments. Racing for the win on the backstretch on the last lap, Johnson was punted from a certain top-three finish when teammate Brian Vickers bumped him as they raced Dale Earnhardt Jr. for the win. Johnson finished 24th.

He couldn't have known it at the moment, but that was the end of Johnson's struggles. The rest of the season would be a virtual yellow brick road – second at Charlotte, first at Martinsville, second at

Atlanta, Texas and Phoenix, and then a solid if unspectacular run in the finale at Homestead.

Knaus addressed the Talladega disappointment almost immediately.

"I can remember walking to the shop the next day, and guys were all bummed out and you could see heads hung pretty low," he said. "I just went around to all of the guys and slapped them on the back and picked them up and said, 'There's a lot going on right now.' I knew we had a lot of opportunities and there

their attitudes were aligned properly entering the final race. Before the season, he had discussed the future of the team with Knaus and Johnson.

"Any time you try hard and you come up a little short—and it was kind of the first time for both of them—they really had to make a decision if they wanted to be together," Hendrick said. "If we were going to come back and compete, Chad had to pace himself. He's the hardest-working guy I've ever seen. He works night and day. I was afraid that Chad was going to burn himself out.

"When things got tough this year, they cinched it up between the two of them.... I'm real proud of them because we went through some pretty tough times and some times where you could point fingers and let the pressure get to you, and they never did this year. I think that's why they rebounded so tough in the Chase, and that's as good of a combination as I've ever had in racing."

Jeff Gordon, who finished sixth in points, agreed to be a co-owner of the No. 48 team when Hendrick added Johnson to his operation. He has been a close friend and adviser to Johnson since Johnson made his Cup debut with three races in 2001.

"I don't like to take much of the credit because Jimmie is a heck of a race-car driver," Gordon said.

In the mid-1990s, Johnson could only dream of standing at the center of attention of America's favorite motorsport. Then, he was racing off-road vehicles and, during the brutal Baja 1000 through the wilds of Mexico, he fell asleep at the wheel, crashed off course and essentially was lost in the desert badlands for most of a day. He had a lot of time to think.

This time, on the other side of the continent, the dreams of a little kid who grew up racing motorcycles came true.

—Mike Hembree

were a lot of opportunities left."

The oh-so-close finishes of the past four seasons, while solid accomplishments for a new team, admittedly created some tension between Johnson and Knaus, who went out of his way during Homestead week to stress that he was feeling no pressure whatsoever with the championship on the line. Team owner Rick Hendrick said he stepped in to smooth the situation and that he talked to the two team principals as late as the night before the race to be sure

GET A GRIP

Johnson Survives Tumultuous Vegas Tilt

UAW-DaimlerChrysler 400 • NASCAR Nextel Cup Race No. 3
March 11, 2007 • Las Vegas, Nev. • Las Vegas Motor Speedway • 267 Laps

Forget the dice, cards and slot machines. Nextel Cup drivers didn't even have to leave the speedway to gamble. The combination of new pavement, increased banking and rock-hard tires forced them to push their luck during the UAW-DaimlerChrysler 400 at Las Vegas Motor Speedway.

Even Jimmie Johnson, who won his third straight race at Las Vegas, never felt at ease on the track.

"It certainly was a fight this weekend to get through it," Johnson said. "I really can't say I had a perfect car and that it was a comfortable drive. You really had to be on your toes all day long and fight hard for it."

While they worked to get the car dialed in, the No. 48 team also had to battle through a brush with the wall and a pit-road penalty. On lap 109, a tire got away during a stop and rolled into an adjoining pit box. NASCAR moved Johnson to the end of the longest line, 25th.

The Lowe's team, just months removed from a championship season, never blinked, and Johnson quickly moved back into contention.

"We had some issues, and these guys really ramp it up when it's 'go time,'" crew chief Chad Knaus, said. "We've got a team full of racers. That's something you don't see on a lot of other teams.

These guys go out there to win races."

The team's first win since they hoisted the Nextel Cup also marked Johnson's 24th victory and Hendrick Motorsports' 150th.

Holding the lead four times for 89 laps, Johnson made a final charge from third around Jeff Gordon and race leader Jeff Burton on lap 240 of the 267-lap race and edged Gordon's No. 24 Hendrick entry by 2.795 seconds.

"The No. 24 had a big advantage on the run before and it seemed like something changed," Johnson said. "We made the right adjustments that helped us out. It really put our car where it needed to be."

Gordon led a race-high 111 laps and left Vegas second in the point standings.

"I'm not going to make excuses; we just basically got beat," he said. "The last lap I made running there behind Jimmie, I was just trying not to spin out coming off the corner. That is how it was for me all day."

Gordon wasn't the only driver struggling to keep his car off the wall. The track-tire combination drew criticism from several of the competitors.

"It was the poorest race I've ever been in," said David Stremme, who started second but finished 20th. "It wasn't fun to drive. A lot of guys were out of control."

Rookie David Ragan was the first to find out just how quickly the car could turn on any driver. Three laps into the race, he slid into the Turn 2 wall, setting the tone for a race slowed by nine cautions.

Running in traffic was particularly treacherous—as tight racing reduced downforce.

"You couldn't run side by side," said fourth-place finisher Matt Kenseth. "When you got along-side of somebody, you were just scared to death you were going to wreck."

Denny Hamlin finished third, and surprise championship leader Mark Martin finished fifth.

With his third consecutive top-five finish and top spot in the standings, Martin tried to head off speculation that he might abandon his plans to run a part-time schedule.

"No change yet," Martin said. "We made this deal, they made the deal and [team owner] Bobby Ginn told me a deal was a deal."

Carl Edwards, Tony Stewart, Ryan Newman, Kyle Busch and Jamie McMurray rounded out the top 10.

Dale Earnhardt Jr. appeared headed for a top-five finish until a late-race miscue. Running fifth on lap 252 when a caution flag flew, he followed Burton onto pit road while the pits were closed. The resulting penalty dropped him to 13th for the restart with 10 laps to go. He picked up two spots to finish 11th.

—Ben White

TITLE TALK

Johnson Eyes Repeat Run

Kobalt Tools 500 • NASCAR Nextel Cup Race No. 4
March 18, 2007 • Hampton, Ga. • Atlanta Motor Speedway • 325 Laps

It's early in the season, but Jimmie Johnson and his No. 48 Hendrick Motorsports team are already thinking championship.

After getting off to a poor start with a 39th-place finish at Daytona, the defending Nextel Cup champion is charging toward the top spot after scoring his second straight win of the young season at Atlanta Motor Speedway.

"After you win a championship, I think it changes you a little bit, and that's what you focus on and what you want to do again and again," Johnson said. "Race wins are a very important step of that, but since we came into '07, the team meetings and discussions, everything we've talked about is trying to win another championship."

Unlike his win a week earlier at Las Vegas, where the team was penalized for a pit miscue, Johnson received top-notch service from his over-the-wall crew at Atlanta.

"It was nice that we've corrected those issues and we're going down a path where we won't have those problems again," crew chief Chad Knaus said. "It was a great win, it was very dramatic, it was very satisfying to go out there and run in the top five all day long and lead some laps and be there at the end. That's what you want to do."

Johnson, who led a race-high 135 laps, had the fastest car, but he had to contend with race leader Tony Stewart down the stretch.

With Johnson charging, Stewart moved to a higher line where he was able to carry more speed through the corner, but the adjustment left Johnson room at the bottom. Johnson made his

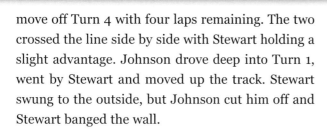

move off Turn 4 with four laps remaining. The two crossed the line side by side with Stewart holding a slight advantage. Johnson drove deep into Turn 1, went by Stewart and moved up the track. Stewart swung to the outside, but Johnson cut him off and Stewart banged the wall.

"When I heard he was there coming, it was just too late for me to adjust, and I certainly squeezed him into the wall and didn't leave him a lot of room," Johnson said. "It wasn't intentional."

Stewart accepted coming up one position short, but he wasn't pleased by Johnson's squeeze move.

"Nobody ever likes to hit the wall. That's pretty much a no-brainer," Stewart said. "I wish he'd have given me a little more room. I don't think I ever pinched him or kept him from having room on the race track to race. He had a faster car. He's probably going to get around us anyway, but I'd like to have seen him give me room to race him for it."

The late-race Johnson-Stewart battle proved to be one of few highlights to an otherwise lackluster event.

Four of the six caution periods on the day were due to debris, while an accident on lap 231 in Turn 3 involved rookie David Reutimann, Kasey Kahne, Greg Biffle and Brian Vickers, the first Toyota driver to lead laps in Nextel Cup competition.

Juan Pablo Montoya impressed the NASCAR veterans by wheeling his Chip Ganassi Racing Dodge to a fifth-place finish behind Johnson, Stewart, Matt Kenseth and Jeff Burton.

Montoya had neither seen nor visited the speedway until Friday's first practice session. During the race, the Colombian rode the high groove.

"When I ran the bottom I think I used a little more wheel," Montoya said. "When you've got a lot of wheel and get on the gas, it gets really loose. When you run the top, you've got a little less wheel. It's probably that, I don't know."

Clint Bowyer finished sixth and was followed by Carl Edwards, Martin Truex Jr., Reed Sorenson and Mark Martin, the points leader who is still determined to run a partial schedule.

"People might not believe it, but they'll have a hard time finding me next week," Martin said. "This thing has really been encompassing. We've worked really hard since January and we've put a lot into this. My team has and I have too. It's been a hard-working stretch and I'm really looking forward to taking a little break."

—Ben White

NO PASSING ZONE

Johnson Holds Off Gordon

Goody's Cool Orange 500 • NASCAR Nextel Cup Race No. 6
April 1, 2007 • Martinsville, Va. • Martinsville Speedway • 500 Laps

When push came to shove at Martinsville Speedway, Jeff Gordon pushed and shoved teammate Jimmie Johnson.

And nothing happened.

In a frantic 50-lap sprint to the finish, Gordon repeatedly bumped, banged and beat up Johnson's car. But the No. 24 still had to settle for runnerup.

The second race with the car of tomorrow revealed that the new car has removed finesse from short track racing.

"I would have been wrecked with last year's car with hits that hard," Johnson said. "Just because the shape of the nose is real round on the old cars and it's like a wedge driving into the back of the car and just lifts the rear tires off the ground.

"These bumpers really hit square, solid. There's no lift. It's just a straight shot in the butt."

Drivers might learn how to pass without wrecking in the car of tomorrow, but in its first two races, second-place drivers were unable to move the leader out of the way tastefully.

Not that Johnson was complaining.

"It seems like the cars are more forgiving right now to contact," he said. "That's a good thing.... The guy in front of you, you can't just go in there and knock him out of the way. You actu-

ally have to drive and try to pass the guy."

While Johnson blocked the No. 24 for those final 50 laps around NASCAR's shortest track, Gordon had to choose between creating controversy by wrecking his Hendrick Motorsports teammate or contenting himself with runnerup status.

"Without wrecking him, there was no way I was going to get it done," Gordon said. "It's one thing to move a guy and use your bumper and a little bit of it is getting experience with these bumpers.

"You've got to really nail the guy and you've got to get him in a really bad position like going into the corner."

The second-place finish was particularly bitter because the No. 24 crew gave their garagemates their fast setup.

After posting the slowest lap in the opening practice a day before the race, Johnson's crew chief, Chad Knaus, asked Gordon's crew chief Steve Letarte for his setup.

"Everything that the 24 car had in it at that point in time, we put into the 48," Knaus said. "We basically said, 'All right, Jimmie buddy, you've got to go out there, Jeff is fast, we need you to try and figure it out.'"

Needless to say, Johnson figured it out. He started

20th but steadily worked his way into the top 10 in fewer than 100 laps. However, he didn't take the lead until lap 388, after which, he led the rest of the race.

With 52 laps remaining, Gordon worked his way to Johnson's tail but that's as far as he would get. He tried to duck inside before he resorted to hammering the back of Johnson's car during the final 10 laps.

"I don't know how he could have hit me much harder," Johnson said. "The way these bumpers line up, I literally put my head up against the head rest just waiting for it. It was coming and it was coming really hard."

Johnson survived the bumps and went home with the trophy. Gordon's car weathered the rough racing, but all Gordon went home with was a second-place check and the points lead.

"I'm mad, but I'm not really mad at him," Gordon said about losing to Johnson. "He didn't do anything wrong. Had I hit him any harder and wrecked them, then the blame would have been put on me and we would have had an issue.

"We don't need that as teammates. We don't need that as competitors going forward trying to win a championship. And I just hope we get our share of wins by continuing to race the way we've been racing."

—Bob Pockrass

COT TO BE KIDDING

No Joke, Hendrick Wins Again

Crown Royal/Jim Stewart 400 • NASCAR Nextel Cup Race No. 10
May 6, 2007 • Richmond, Va. • Richmond International Raceway • 400 Laps

It's safe to say that Hendrick Motorsports' car of tomorrow program is well ahead of the competition following Jimmie Johnson's victory in the Crown Royal/Jim Stewart 400 at Richmond International Raceway.

That's four COT races and four wins for Hendrick — all in a car that was predicted by some to be the great equalizer.

Johnson raced past teammate Kyle Busch with 20 laps remaining and held on to win while fellow Hendrick driver Jeff Gordon finished fourth.

"I am surprised to see, at the end of the day, Hendrick's still at the front and we're taking trophies home," Johnson said. "But we have a lot of competition. There are things that have been eliminating people from fighting for the win. That's one thing I've been real proud of my team. Our pit stops just get stronger throughout the day. Chad [Knaus, crew chief] is amazing with strategy and not getting us in a hole."

Despite the new car, Hendrick teams have followed the strategy that has earned them 156 Cup wins: fast cars and few mistakes.

"We're as good as they are — we're better at times, we're worse at times," said Joe Gibbs Racing's Denny Hamlin, who finished third and ran behind the Hendrick cars throughout the race. "They've got all the wins because they haven't made any mistakes. I've made mistakes. My pit crew has made mistakes."

And the rain delay could have opened the door for an upset. Heavy rains on Saturday night forced

NASCAR to move the race to Sunday afternoon, putting the race under sunny skies and changing every team's setup.

Nevertheless, the Hendrick Motorsports stable was stout. Gordon had the best car at the start of the race, leading the most laps (114) of any driver.

However, the competition rallied. Richard Childress Racing's Kevin Harvick led 105 laps and likely would have battled for the win if not for an accident on pit road.

Johnson, who started fourth, led most of his laps late in the event. He and Busch combined to pace the field for the final 121 circuits.

The No. 48 assumed the lead when Penske Racing's Kurt Busch — another driver with a potential race-winning car — pitted, came out ninth and never again challenged for the lead.

"Once we got to the end, I knew where I needed to be," Johnson said.

If the Chase began after 10 races, Johnson's four wins would give him a 40-point bonus and the points lead. Gordon, with two wins, would sit 20 points behind. And, by the way, five of the 10 Chase races are COT events.

"I know the car of tomorrow is a big part of our sport now, and it's just something we need to stay on top of along with the current cars," Johnson said. "I'm excited that we're going to have a good mix of those races. But it's so far from now, there's no telling what technology is going to come along, what the cars are going to be wanting, [such as] tires.

"We're doing the right things now, and we're going to focus in on the next six or seven months to stay on top of things."

—Bob Pockrass

HEATING UP

Johnson Steams into Chase

Sharp Aquos 500 • NASCAR Nextel Cup Race No. 25
Sept. 2, 2007 • Fontana, Calif. • California Speedway • 250 Laps

Jimmie Johnson was itching to get back to victory lane heading into the Sharp Aquos 500 at California Speedway.

While the Hendrick Motorsports driver was safely among the top 10 in points, he had not won a race since May and knew that defending his 2006 championship hinged upon a strong pre-Chase charge.

So before heading out to the West Coast, Johnson and crew chief Chad Knaus hunkered down with the No. 48 crew and put all of their efforts into leaving California with a win.

"We really wanted to win this race," Knaus said. "Fontana has been a good track for us."

True enough. Johnson drove to victory in 2002 and has never finished worse than 16th at the 2-mile superspeedway. However, the car Knaus fancied for the race had to be rebuilt after it was wrecked in a fierce crash at Chicagoland Speedway.

"I really felt very confident with this race car," Knaus said. "It's only finished out of the top two twice. It's a great car, and I wanted to bring it back."

With the rebuilt car, Johnson qualified on the outside of the front row despite sweltering conditions that pushed track temperatures beyond the 140-degree mark. That same furnace-like heat greeted the drivers, crews and fans on race day, yet an estimated 80,000 spectators turned out for the 500-mile race — 15,000 shy of a sellout but impressive given the extreme heat.

Polesitter Kurt Busch led the field to the green

flag as Johnson settled in among the top five and patiently worked with Knaus to improve the handling on the No. 48 Chevrolet.

However, as the sun set, Johnson made his way to the front while several frontrunners faded.

"As the track changed, we made small changes and got better and better," Johnson said. "The car was by far at its best late in the race."

Following the final round of pit stops, Johnson led the way with teammate Kyle Busch and Carl Edwards nipping at his heels.

Busch, who led a race-high 97 laps, pushed Johnson, but Edwards proved to be the real threat — moving around Busch and into second with 10 laps remaining.

Edwards upped his pace, but Johnson countered with a series of fast laps and held off the Roush Fenway driver to score the win. Busch finished third and was followed by Jeff Burton and Dale Earnhardt Jr.

"I forgot about the 99 [Edwards] back there. I thought the 5 [Busch] was in second place," Johnson said. "I saw the 99 there, went back to the bottom of the track and gained some time."

Watching Johnson pull away was especially painful for Edwards, who was certain he could steal the win.

"It looked to me like Jimmie was searching [for a better groove]," Edwards said. "He was a little slow. I thought he was going to be a sitting duck. I even said to Bob [Osborne, crew chief] on the radio, 'I feel like it's me and Kyle racing for the win here.' Running second is terrible."

With a series-leading five wins — each worth 10 points come Chase-time — Johnson is assured of starting the 10-race playoff in at least a tie for the top spot, which has the California native confident about his chances to repeat as champion.

"There is obviously a lot of racing left and a lot of good teams fighting for the Chase, but we are hitting our stride at the right time," Johnson said. "It's time for the pressure to pick up and my guys are ready for it."

—Jon Gunn

ROCKING AND ROLLING

Johnson Surges, Earnhardt Jr. Fades

Chevy Rock & Roll 400 • NASCAR Nextel Cup Race No. 26
Sept. 8, 2007 • Richmond, Va. • Richmond International Raceway • 400 Laps

While all eyes focused on Kevin Harvick, Kurt Busch and Dale Earnhardt Jr., who were battling to make the Chase, Jimmie Johnson dominated the Chevy Rock & Roll 400 at Richmond International Raceway.

Johnson didn't seem to mind sharing the spotlight, however. Like nine other drivers, he was locked into the Chase and made the most of a night when he could afford to race without worrying about points. He and Hendrick Motorsports teammate Jeff Gordon sent a message to the field by leading a combined 295 of 400 laps — with Johnson out front for the final 61 circuits.

With his second consecutive victory and sixth of the 2007 season, Johnson claimed the top spot in the Chase standings with 60 bonus points to Gordon's 40.

While Gordon dominated early in the race, Johnson was on cruise control by lap 340.

"The race was starting off good for us and we ran in the top five all night," Johnson said. "At the end, the car started to come to life. Adjustments were spot-on and got me in good track position. The last 100 laps, the car was as good as it's been.

"We're happy to be hitting our stride at this point in the season. As everybody knows, it was a little bit of a tough summer for us. But everything is working right now."

Tony Stewart led 27 laps and held off rookie David Ragan for second. Gordon finished fourth and was followed by Johnny Sauter, Denny Hamlin, Harvick, Kasey Kahne, Busch and J.J. Yeley.

Harvick needed only to finish 32nd or better to clinch a Chase spot, and a lap-243 accident threatened to push the Daytona 500 winner out of NASCAR's "postseason."

The No. 29 had to scramble through the grass to avoid being collected in the wreck, which started when Ryan Newman spun in front of Juan Pablo Montoya. Harvick's car suffered no damage, but grass clogged the radiator vents, causing the engine to overheat.

Fortunately, his crew members cured the problem easily by wiping the debris away during the next pit stop.

"The way these cars are, it's like a shovel with the splitter on the bottom of the car," Harvick said. "It just filled the grill up solid and there was water coming out. Once we got that off, it actually ran cooler than it had earlier in the race."

Meanwhile, Busch, needing to finish 36th or better, suffered heavy damage to the back of his car in the same crash that threatened Harvick. Crew members pulled away the bent sheet metal, and the Penske Racing driver returned to the race.

"I saw my teammate get loose or spun out and there was smoke everywhere," Busch said. "The best thing I could have done was just stop and hunker down and wait for the impact.

"Our hearts were beating a thousand miles per hour after that because I figured the rear bumper cover was flapping in the wind or there might be material dragging on the tires. Luckily, there was a red flag at that point. We checked the car out and everything was OK."

Earnhardt, hoping for a miracle, needed to win and lead the most laps to edge Busch and Harvick. Driving hard all night, he challenged Stewart for

second near the end, but the sixth engine failure of the season sent him to the garage.

"We're just very disappointed for the engine failures to take us physically out of the Chase," Earnhardt said. "We've run in the top five every week, and my team is very upset and disappointed and bummed about it."

While Earnhardt consoled his team and looked forward to the 2008 campaign, Johnson, the reigning Nextel Cup champion, was ready for the 10-race championship fight.

"I think my mental strength is much greater than what it was last year. I also think the team is stronger," Johnson said. "Experience helps everyone on so many levels in motorsports and I think life in general. But to be able to go through the five seasons of almost getting it, the letdown and then getting it last year and knowing that we can do it, we've been there and we can fight through this."

—Ben White

SEIZING CONTROL

Johnson Extends Chase Lead with Dominant Win

Subway 500 • NASCAR Nextel Cup Race No. 32
Oct. 21, 2007 • Martinsville, Va. • Martinsville Speedway • 506 Laps

Jimmie Johnson made the Chase For The Nextel Cup a two-car race by winning the Subway 500 at Martinsville Speedway.

The victory marked the third straight and fourth overall for Johnson at the Nextel Cup tour's shortest track. Third-place finisher Jeff Gordon even visited victory lane to label him "Mr. Martinsville."

Richard Petty (15 Martinsville wins) might argue that point, but there is no question Johnson has had a headlock on Martinsville in recent years.

Oddly enough, Johnson had every chance to let the win slip away on this latest visit. Gordon, hoping to win for the third straight week, and second-place finisher Ryan Newman, winless since 2005, took shots at him in the twilight laps. Meanwhile, wacky driving produced a staggering 21 caution flags (a track record) and 127 caution laps (another track record). Fully one-quarter of the race was run under yellow, including, quite naturally, the finish.

The day's next-to-last caution forced the race into extra laps, and it finally ended at lap 506, making it the longest race in Martinsville's 60-year history. The checkered flag, accompanied by the yellow, fell 15 seconds short of four hours, as shadows spread across the speedway on a beautiful autumn afternoon.

The end was shaping up nicely as Johnson and

Gordon settled into first and second place and promised to duplicate the wild 1-2 finish they scored here on April Fools' Day. In the spring race, Johnson frustrated Gordon as they bumped and banged side by side through Turn 4 to the finish.

They tried their best to produce a sequel, but the flagman wouldn't let them. Time after time, they roared into Turn 1 bumper to bumper. Then, with the crowd preparing to hold its collective breath, a caution — for oil sprayed on the track, for a three-car wreck on the backstretch, for spin after spin after spin, for a concession stand spreading too much mustard on a hot dog — would interrupt the drama.

It was yellow fever at its best. Or its worst.

Johnson and Gordon appeared set to settle it when the green flag fell on lap 491, but Newman, largely silent this season, bumped Gordon and moved into second place, angering Gordon and earning a retaliatory thump. Then, a three-car wreck put the yellow out again on lap 497, and the cleanup forced extra laps.

Johnson led Newman and Gordon to the day's final green flag, but any chance of real racing fizzled when David Ragan spun in Turn 1 and wound up sideways low on the track. Officials tried to give Ragan time to move but finally put out the caution and ended the race.

Johnson won for a series-leading seventh time this season.

"The circumstances were different," Johnson said, comparing the Subway 500 finish to the spring race. "I was chasing him [Gordon] down at the end and was able to get by him. So I didn't have the same set of emotions as I did in the spring race, where he was actually a little better than us at reeling us in, and I was just kind of up there hanging on."

The race had little impact on the Chase outside of drawing Gordon and Johnson closer. Gordon, the leader, entered the day 68 points in front of the

No. 48. However, Johnson could only narrow the gap by 15 points. Meanwhile, third-place Clint Bowyer, who finished ninth at Martinsville, sat 115 behind Gordon.

"I'm very, very pleased to come out of here with a third-place finish, considering what could have happened," Gordon said.

The Johnson-Gordon confrontation that was seemingly inevitable at the end of the race was turned upside down by Newman, who isn't in the Chase and has had only five top-fives this year.

"We had a little bump-and-run there with the 24 [of Gordon]," Newman said. "That is something that has happened to me in the past, so I didn't feel that bad giving it to him."

Although the bump-and-run is generally accepted at Martinsville, Gordon didn't appreciate Newman's move.

"He said he got in too hot and made a mistake," Gordon said. "That mistake almost cost us the race. We talked about it when the race was over. It's a dropped issue, and we'll move on."

Meanwhile, Johnson was more than happy to avoid another late-race battle with his teammate.

"There is no one that we want to beat more than the No. 24," Johnson said. "We know what they have. We know how good they are. And they make us step up week after week.

"Today, we raced hard. We leaned on each other from time to time, but in the end he came over to victory lane. I can't say how much that impressed me. The last two weeks he won, my bottom lip was dragging the ground so hard I couldn't even make it to victory lane to congratulate him, and then the guy comes over and congratulates me. So, he's certainly a class act and a great leader for Hendrick Motorsports."

—Mike Hembree

SURPRISE, SURPRISE

Title Contender Johnson Earns Eighth Win

Pep Boys Auto 500 • NASCAR Nextel Cup Race No. 33
Oct. 28, 2007 • Hampton, Ga. • Atlanta Motor Speedway • 329 Laps

Things didn't get interesting in the Pep Boys Auto 500 at Atlanta Motor Speedway until the final two laps when Jimmie Johnson emerged as the surprise winner.

It came as a surprise because Johnson hadn't run up front for much of the day. But after crew chief Chad Knaus called for two tires on the final pit stop, Johnson suddenly found himself in contention for the win.

Denny Hamlin led the way on a restart with two laps to go, but he slowed suddenly, dropped low on the track and chaos erupted behind him.

Martin Truex Jr., running second, slammed into Hamlin, and Johnson squirted by on the high side to claim the lead with soon-to-be Hendrick Motorsports teammate Dale Earnhardt Jr. in second.

Earnhardt had a real shot to end a 58-race winless streak, but he lost a wheel and spun into the wall on lap 328.

"Man, that was a hit," Earnhardt said. "It was hard and loud — bam into the wall. I knew when I was sliding up there it was gonna be big and it was."

The race ended under caution with Johnson leading Carl Edwards, Reed Sorenson, Matt Kenseth and Jeff Burton.

Aside from earning a season-leading eighth win of the year, Johnson moved within nine points of Chase leader and Hendrick Motorsports teammate, Jeff Gordon.

"I still think that it's going to be a fight to the end," Johnson said. "We took a good bite out of Jeff's point lead today, and it's going to come down to a position or two in the next three races. I feel really good about where we are in the points."

One driver who wasn't feeling good was Hamlin. His battered car was found to have been running on a mixture of fuel and water — as were the cars of several other drivers.

"All day we had been getting water in our fuel," Hamlin said. "The water displaces fuel, and so we weren't getting the full potential of fuel. We took it apart again [after the race] and pulled some gas out of the fuel cell and again we get water.

"It's a shame. Once again, it wasn't our day."

Whether the water problem prevented him from accelerating is unclear, according to Joe Gibbs Racing Senior Vice President Jimmy Makar.

Nextel Cup Series Director John Darby said no water was found in the Sunoco gas pumps following the race. He said NASCAR didn't know how the water got into the fuel cells.

"What we do kind of believe is that it may have came on the very first fill of the day," Darby said. "Water settles to the bottom [of the tank].

"But just as soon as you move enough gallons of fuel through anything, then it's liable to flush out and be clean. That's what we're trying to find out — the sequence of the cans that got filled this morning."

The crew chiefs of the afflicted teams were perplexed. "We had water in our fuel from the get-go, all day," said Dave Blaney's crew chief Tommy Baldwin. "We put [the car] back in the garage and worked on it and didn't know what was going on. We drained it — half water and half fuel."

Baldwin said the fuel still had water in it at the end of the race, but he didn't know for sure how that happened.

"There might have been some remnants still in there," Baldwin said. "I'm guessing we were probably one of the first ones to get fuel — us and the [No.] 11 [Hamlin] this morning or something. We're trying to find out the chain of events now."

—Kris Johnson

HOT SHOT
Johnson Storms to Victory at Texas

Dickies 500 • NASCAR Nextel Cup Race No. 34
Nov. 4, 2007 • Fort Worth, Texas • Texas Motor Speedway • 334 Laps

Jimmie Johnson's late-season surge continued at Texas Motor Speedway, as the Hendrick Motorsports driver moved to the top of the Chase standings with his third straight victory and ninth of the season.

Kyle Busch had been the star of the Dickies 500 show, leading a race-high 153 laps, until Johnson passed him on pit road on the final stop with 29 laps to go.

While the No. 48 took four tires, three cars ahead of Johnson — Ryan Newman, Matt Kenseth and Jamie McMurray — took two tires each. Nevertheless the No. 48 quickly passed the Newman/McMurray duo on the restart.

That freed Johnson to set his sights on leader Kenseth, though he still trailed by 1.5 seconds with just over 20 laps to go.

No matter. Johnson sliced the lead to a half-second within four laps and began to stalk the No. 17.

But Kenseth did not plan on rolling over. The two drivers waged what Johnson described as "a full-blown brawl."

With six laps to go, they crossed the start/finish line in a dead heat. But Kenseth had better positioning, and Johnson had to momentarily back off.

Still, Kenseth knew he couldn't hold Johnson off to the checkered flag.

"He ran me down from a long way back," Kenseth said. "I don't know how fast he was, but I was steadily losing grip. Four tires are just too much."

Three laps later, Johnson noticed that Kenseth was leaving him the bottom groove.

That, Johnson said, "let me understand that his stuff was starting to tighten up. The two tires weren't working, and he was running for defense rather than offense."

Those older tires just wouldn't hold off Johnson any longer, and the No. 48 Chevy drove to the front on lap 332 and took the win.

Kenseth held onto second and Martin Truex Jr., Busch and Newman followed.

"All right, boys!" Johnson yelled on the team radio. "Let's go win a Cup!"

Wait a minute. What happened to the whole concept of points racing?

Johnson had little to gain and much more to lose by racing aggressively for the win.

Sure, he wouldn't have gotten 15 extra points and would have lost out on the chance to wear a cowboy hat and shoot pistols in the air during the Texas-style victory celebration. But was it worth the risk of wrecking and letting teammate Jeff Gordon

maintain the points lead and gain a big advantage?

"At times, I thought about the points," Johnson said.

"But Jeff was getting better as the night went on, and I knew I needed every point I could get and I had to go for it.

"Every spot counts. You've got to go for it, and that's what I was doing tonight."

Johnson emerged from the late-race battle with a 30-point lead over Gordon, who had led the standings since Talladega.

"It's still close, but they're spanking us," Gordon said. "They're putting it to us. I don't like it. We're very competitive and we're just getting beat.

"Here they are with three in a row, and they're on a great roll. We've got to answer back. That's all there is to it."

Surprise Chase contender Clint Bowyer, third in points, made two unscheduled green-flag stops beginning on lap 245 to correct a mysterious tire vibration, falling two laps down to finish 19th. The miscue dropped him 181 points behind Johnson and all but out of championship contention.

"We are down but not out in the Chase," Bowyer said. "There is no give up in this team. We are going to take it a lap at a time, race at a time and keep fighting until the checkered flag falls at Homestead."

—Ben White

UNSTOPPABLE

Johnson's Domination Continues at Phoenix

Checker Auto Parts 500 • NASCAR Nextel Cup Race No. 35
Nov. 11, 2007 • Phoenix, Ariz. • Phoenix International Raceway • 312 Laps

There's no stopping Jimmie Johnson. The Hendrick Motorsports driver made that clear at Phoenix International Raceway — where he took a commanding lead in the Chase For The Nextel Cup after winning his fourth straight race and 10th of the season.

Asked to describe his phenomenal streak, Johnson was at a loss. "I don't have a clue. I just go out, do my job, just do the best I can," he said. "I am shaking my head. I don't know what to think about the success we have had this year. I cannot believe 10 wins in one year. It is unbelievable."

The turning point for Johnson came on lap 272 of 312 — during the day's 10th caution period.

Martin Truex Jr. and Johnny Sauter did not pit and ran first and second, while Matt Kenseth, Tony Stewart, Johnson and a handful of other drivers took two tires.

After the green flag came out on lap 275, Johnson was already pressuring Kenseth for second by lap 278. When Kenseth got hemmed in behind the slower car of Aric Almirola, Johnson slid by. Less than 10 laps later, he had Truex in his sights.

"Our car was really good on two tires," Johnson said. "The No. 17 [Kenseth] and No. 20 [Stewart] had gotten two tires two stops in a row, so it was the right call. Truex was out there on old tires, so the perfect scenario came together for us to take advantage of."

Johnson dropped his No. 48 Chevrolet on the low side of the track coming out of Turn 2 on lap 289 and was side by side with Truex on the backstretch.

Coming out of Turn 4, Johnson grabbed the lead and held the top spot for the rest of the way.

Greg Biffle finished 0.870 second behind Johnson, and Kenseth finished third ahead of Stewart, Ryan Newman, Kevin Harvick, Truex, Kyle Busch, Jeff Burton and Jeff Gordon.

"We just needed Jimmie to make a little mistake, and we could have been on him," Biffle said. "But those guys are pretty good at not making mistakes."

Kenseth concurred.

"They're just unbelievably good," he said. "They're as good as any group I've seen — including Jeff [Gordon] in his heyday when he was winning 10 races a year and the championship by over a hundred points."

Johnson's recent success all but erased Gordon's hopes for securing a fifth Cup championship. His 10th-place finish left him 86 points behind Johnson heading into the season finale at Homestead-Miami Speedway.

"It's over," Gordon said of the championship. "Even if we win it, it's because they have problems. While we would accept it, we don't want to do it that way. Those guys have flat-out killed everybody. We

didn't step up when we needed to. We gave them a run for a while. Now, we have to figure out how to get the best finish we can at Homestead and end the season on a positive note going to the offseason.

"I thought this was our year to get another one, and we're just coming up short here at the crucial time. Those guys have just knocked it out of the ballpark. It's going to be tough to beat them even if we were hitting on all eight cylinders. It's another

top-10 but still just not good enough to get it done."

Even with the championship virtually locked up, Johnson wasn't ready to proclaim victory.

"I need every point," he said. "There's no telling how things will go in Homestead. If we put our guard down and don't try to score maximum points every week, we're going to get beat. That's just how good he [Gordon] and that team is."

—Ben White

AN EXCELLENT STUDENT

Jimmie Johnson Learned from the Best to Become NASCAR's Top Driver

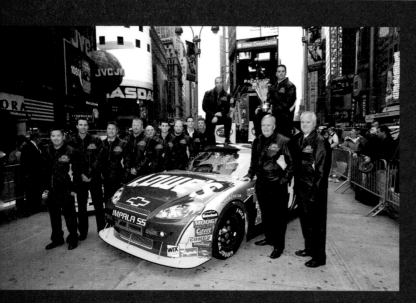

Jimmie Johnson isn't the spitting image of Hendrick Motorsports teammate Jeff Gordon, but it's evident that, on the race track at least, there aren't many differences between the two.

Johnson, 32, is now a two-time Nextel Cup champion. Gordon, 36, is a four-time champ. Johnson won 10 times in 2007 en route to the title, eventually besting Gordon, a six-time race winner this year himself.

The first driver to win four consecutive races since Gordon in 1998, Johnson's 10 wins were also the most in a single season since his teammate won 13 in '98.

Gordon may have enjoyed more success—from 1995 through 1999 he won seven or more races each season—but Johnson and crew chief Chad Knaus have now won three or more races for six consecutive years.

It's no wonder fellow competitors look at the two teams and see striking similarities.

"When I think of Jimmie and Chad and the things that they've been able to do, I really think of Jeff Gordon and [former crew chief] Ray Evernham when they were winning all those races," says Roush Fenway Racing's Matt Kenseth. "That's really who they remind me of."

Gordon was already the established star, Johnson the up-and-coming student when the two became teammates in 2001. Six years later, it's obvious Johnson has staked his own claim to his lofty position in the sport. Graduation day has come and gone.

It's the era of JJ.

Team owner Rick Hendrick has been there for the ascension of both Gordon and Johnson. And while he isn't ready to write off the driver of his

team's No. 24 Chevrolet, he understands that it is Johnson who currently holds the upper hand. He notes the aggressiveness and intelligence of both Johnson and Knaus, qualities he's seen in others who have enjoyed similar success when paired together.

"His talent and the way he approached racing, the fact that he goes Monday morning and works out after a race on Sunday, he's as determined as anybody I've ever seen sit down in a race car," Hendrick says of Johnson.

Teacher And Pupil

He watched. He listened. He learned. Johnson was given the equipment to succeed as soon as he became a member of the Hendrick Motorsports fold. Cars that carried Gordon to the 2001 championship

were refurbished, and served as the building blocks for the organization's newest team.

But it was Johnson's attentiveness that helped rocket him through the Cup learning curve at warp speed. Despite his inexperience, he matched his mentor win for win in 2002 and 2003. He's exceeded Gordon's win total every year since. And he's won two titles while Gordon has continued to chase that elusive No. 5.

He's been able to accomplish much of that, Johnson says, primarily because of his teammate's unselfishness.

"I've always had someone to look up to, and to try to learn from coming into Hendrick Motorsports, Jeff was certainly that for me. I feel it's been good for me," Johnson says. "I've been so trained to look at my

problems put his car in the wall.

Johnson was devastated. Knaus, refusing to delegate responsibilities, was distraught. Neither wanted to give up, but each knew something had to change.

"I'm not going to sugarcoat it. We were frustrated with each other," Johnson says. "But the thing we always had is that we believed in one another. I didn't want a new crew chief and he didn't want another driver. But it just wasn't working."

The end result was that Johnson would provide more of a voice for the team while Knaus would learn to spread the various responsibilities surrounding the running of the team among others in the organization.

"I'm sure from Rick's standpoint he thought that a great thing was falling apart," Johnson says. "But Chad and I never lost belief."

Twice Is Nice

With back-to-back titles, the second coming after a brilliant performance in the Chase, Johnson is at the top of his game.

Terry Labonte, a former Hendrick teammate who retired at the end of the 2006 season, says he isn't surprised by Johnson's success.

"I told Rick it's hard for anyone to realize just how good Jimmie is as a driver," Labonte, a two-time champion, says. "I think the 2006 championship gave the team the confidence it needed, and in 2007 they were able to turn in a dominating performance."

Johnson knows securing back-to-back titles puts him in elite company – only nine others have won consecutive championships. And only one, Cale Yarborough (1976-78), has captured three in a row.

"Hopefully, we can be a three-time champion in the near future," Johnson says.

—Kenny Bruce

teammates' driving style and what they do, that under the last five or six years I've been studying Jeff and his driving style and I've learned a lot from that."

Gordon was impressed with Johnson, he says, before he ever saw the former off-road racer climb behind the wheel of a stock car.

What could a guy with that much raw talent do, he wondered, if he was given the right opportunity?

"I really thought if we put him in the kind of car and equipment that I had been in for all these years, that he could have the same type of success that I had," Gordon says. "And to me, he has the capability of having more success."

A Bump In The Road

Of course, it wasn't always smooth sailing for Johnson. Coming so close to the championship – he finished second in 2003 and '04 before slipping to fifth in 2005 – proved to be mentally taxing. At the end of the '05 season, it had reached a boiling point.

Trailing series leader Tony Stewart by just 52 points heading into the season finale at Homestead, Johnson finished a disappointing 40th after tire

PHOTO GALLERY

"Since I was a kid, I just wanted to race. I wanted to be the best at racing. I didn't know where it would lead me or what was in store for me or where it would go, but I love to race."

"I believe in my guys, believe in myself,
believe in the team, and let's just go racing."

"We've done a lot of great things. It's hard to believe in some ways it seems like the eight years have flown by, in other ways it seems longer. But it's been a very, very special eight years. I'm thankful that Lowe's took that chance with me years back."

TRIPLE CROWN 2000

BACK ON TOP
Johnson, Knaus Return to Victory Lane

Subway Fresh Fit 500 • NASCAR Sprint Cup Race No. 8
April 12, 2008 • Phoenix, Ariz. • Phoenix International Raceway • 312 Laps

If this is what a slump looks like at Hendrick Motorsports, the rest of the field could be in for a long 2008.

"Rebounding" from an eight-race winless streak, the No. 48 team reasserted itself, closing out the Subway Fresh Fit 500 on a fuel-mileage gamble that put them back in victory lane.

An 82-lap green-flag run ended the race and tested the fuel mileage of every car in the field. Only a handful of laps from the checkered flag, leaders

Mark Martin and Denny Hamlin were forced to pit for fuel. Jimmie Johnson, running in third, inherited the lead and sailed to an easy win.

With Hamlin and Martin out of the way, Johnson could lay back and rely on a nearly 10-second advantage over second-place Clint Bowyer. So, he lifted off the throttle, all but coasting around the track over the last couple of laps.

"I just tried to stay up in the second lane, be smart with the fuel and not step on the gas pedal too hard," Johnson said.

Though it might be tempting to write this one off as a fuel-mileage win—attributing the victory to the fickle racing fates or implying that once again a Hendrick team got all the good fortune—make no mistake, this race did not come as easily as it may have looked.

Johnson started that last run mired in traffic and had to work his way through the field to be in position for the win.

"I'm shocked that I was able to save fuel running that hard up through the field," he said. "I restarted in 14th on that last restart and drove to third on my own, and then I got to the front and was able to manage some fuel."

Crew chief Chad Knaus underscored the fact that

the No. 48 didn't luck into its first victory of 2008.

"We didn't win it on fuel mileage," Knaus said. "If everybody came down pit road and took four tires, I think we still would have been in position to race for the win."

And from the looks of it, Knaus was right. Johnson picked up where he left off last season at Phoenix — winning the last of his four straight wins that catapulted him to the 2007 championship.

Starting seventh, Johnson snatched the lead from polesitter Ryan Newman on lap 31. Though he would briefly trade the lead with Newman and his teammate Dale Earnhardt Jr., Johnson dominated the first half of the race, leading 119 of the first 149 laps.

Then, Newman, running in the top 10, blew an engine seal and threw Knaus a curveball. After a nearly 10-minute red-flag to clean up fluid put down by the No. 12, Knaus made the call to stay out while the rest of the field pitted. The decision nearly cost the team the win.

"If I hadn't botched it up," Knaus said, "we'd have been up front all day. It was just that one pit call got us relegated to the back."

After not pitting, a caution seven laps later forced Knaus' hand.

"We had to pit.... Obviously, everybody else stayed out. We had to line up at 17th or something.... We were just kind of trapped in the back for quite a while."

While Johnson chipped away at the lead, Earnhardt charged to the front. Battling Martin for most of the second half of the race, Earnhardt led 87 laps, second to Johnson's 120.

But when it mattered most, Junior's car failed him.

"It was like someone flipped a switch there at the end and the tires were gone."

Hamlin went on to finish third with Carl Edwards and Martin trailing. Jeff Burton hung on to the points lead with a sixth-place finish. Earnhardt, Martin Truex Jr., Greg Biffle and Kyle Busch rounded out the top 10.

—Jay Pfeifer

GOOD GRIEF

Pitiful Goodyear Rubber Spoils Indy

Allstate 400 at The Brickyard • NASCAR Sprint Cup Race No. 20
July 27, 2008 • Indianapolis, Ind. • Indianapolis Motor Speedway • 160 Laps

---

Jimmie Johnson won the Allstate 400 — 10 laps at a time. However, Johnson's efforts at the famed Indianapolis Motor Speedway won't be what people remember.

Sure, the driver of the No. 48 Hendrick Motorsports Chevrolet left with the trophy, a check for a half-million dollars, and the satisfaction that his team is hitting its stride. But the 15th running of the 400 will go down as a fiasco wrought by poor planning and a tire unsuitable for the track and NASCAR's new car.

Goodyear conducted a tire test at the 2.5-mile track earlier in the year, but issues with the rubber cropped up during practice two days before the race. They intensified on the eve of the 400 when crews discovered the right rear tires showing an alarmingly high rate of wear after just eight to 10 laps.

The situation wasn't new to IMS, which was hosting NASCAR's new car for the first time, but it was more pronounced. In previous years, the track had eventually built up enough rubber from race traffic that it became a non-issue. This year, there was no such build-up.

As a result, NASCAR ordered six mandatory "competition caution" periods so that teams could monitor tire wear. Combined with three cautions

for actual racing incidents and two more for blown right rear tires, fans never saw more than 13 laps of consecutive green-flag racing.

Johnson and crew chief Chad Knaus rolled with the punches and waited until the perfect moment to make their move — during the final pit stop on lap 151 of 160.

The strategy paid off in spades. Third behind Denny Hamlin and Elliott Sadler when the final

caution appeared, Johnson beat everyone off pit road to take the lead for the final seven-lap charge.

Carl Edwards, who emerged in second, fought Johnson for the win but came up 0.332-second short. Hamlin finished third, and Sadler and Jeff Gordon rounded out the top five.

"Carl put a lot of pressure on me at the end

there," Johnson said. "I have to commend him, how hard he was driving. I think it was a good race there at the end.

"I can honestly say nobody wanted to be in this position. I commend NASCAR in handling today like they did. NASCAR called a great race."

Ryan Newman, who finished 13th, didn't share

Johnson's view.

"It wasn't a race today. It's ridiculous," he said. "That's a lack of preparation from NASCAR to Goodyear to the Indianapolis Motor Speedway to put on a show like they did for the fans today. It's disrespectful to the fans. That's not the way NASCAR racing is supposed to be."

Newman might have been upset, but at least he avoided problems on the track. Matt Kenseth brought out the day's fourth caution when his right rear tire blew on the backstretch and tore his car apart.

"This is one of the two biggest races of the year, and...it's pretty darn disappointing," Kenseth said. "I feel bad for the fans. We're running three-quarters speed because we're worried about the tires blowing out, and they got blown out every eight laps."

Robin Pemberton, NASCAR vice president of competition, spent the majority of the race on pit road studying tire wear, attempting to gauge whether the problem was getting better or worse.

"Based on what we dealt with here last year and year before last, we felt like [the tire] was going to come to us by race day, and it didn't happen," Pemberton said. "We're here to put on the best races we can, and we do a damn good job of that most of the time. Everybody inside these walls works real hard to do that."

—**Kenny Bruce**

NO LOOKING BACK

Johnson Crushes Field as Chase Approaches

Pepsi 500 • NASCAR Sprint Cup Race No. 25
Aug. 31, 2008 • Fontana, Calif. • Auto Club Speedway • 250 Laps

Despite starting from the pole and absolutely crushing the field in the Pepsi 500 — had this been little league baseball, the umps would have called it halfway through — Jimmie Johnson didn't even lead the first lap.

Instead, outside polesitter AJ Allmendinger, enjoying his highest-ever starting position, nosed across the start/finish line just ahead of the No. 48. But then Johnson took over, leading 228 of the remaining 249 laps.

And looking back, it seems more likely that

Allmendinger's brief surge was less a demonstration of a superior car than an act of charity or a display of supreme nonchalance by the No. 48.

Go ahead, take it. I don't need it.

His victory was so total that it surprised even Johnson — a driver who has seen victory lane 36 times in his seven-year career.

"I think this is the most dominant car and victory that we've ever had," Johnson said.

In a suspense-free race, Johnson, crew chief Chad Knaus and team owner Rick Hendrick led by so much that they worried more about a freak occurrence or an equipment failure than any of the 42 other cars on the track.

"Usually, when you are that good, you wait for something to happen," Hendrick said. "When you have a car that good, it's hard to capitalize on a race."

But nothing went wrong.

While the No. 48 crew held its collective breath, Greg Biffle tried to make it a race. The driver of the No. 16 Ford did manage to lead five times for 12 laps but could never pass Johnson on the track. Instead, Biffle tasted clean air thanks to a crisp pit crew.

"They were the fastest guys on pit road tonight and I've never had that before in my life," Biffle said. "It feels pretty good to beat everybody off of

pit road time and time again."

But Johnson quickly snuffed all of Biffle's brief forays out front.

Even when his competitors tried to get cute — taking two tires while the No. 48 changed all four — Johnson never faltered. On a lap 162 pit stop, five cars leapfrogged Johnson and pushed him out of the top five for the first time of the evening. But with fresh rubber and an unbeatable car, Johnson reclaimed the lead just seven laps later.

"I thought it was going to take longer myself," Johnson said. "But I went through Turns 1 and 2 and I'm just flying by people and I started smiling, like, OK, this won't take long. And we were back to the front."

He would repeat that scenario several more times before crossing the stripe over two seconds ahead of Biffle.

Johnson and the No. 48 crew seemed to be finding their championship form just in time.

"I'm happy to win and win on a big track because the bulk of the races [in the Chase] are on these big downforce tracks. I feel like we're doing the right things to have a fighting chance at the championship," Johnson said.

Johnson was one of three drivers who clinched a 2008 Chase berth. Dale Earnhardt Jr. and Jeff Burton will also join him in the 10-race playoff. Biffle, Denny Hamlin, Kevin Harvick and Matt Kenseth rounded out the top five and shored up their Chase prospects.

Meanwhile, three drivers locked in a pitched battle for the last Chase berth kept it close. Kasey Kahne finished ninth but couldn't climb out of 14th place because Clint Bowyer finished 10th to hang on to the final spot in the Chase while David Ragan hung in at 13th in points with a 13th-place run.

—Jay Pfeifer

MAKING HIS MOVE

Johnson Zooms into Chase with Richmond Win

Chevy Rock & Roll 400 • NASCAR Sprint Cup Race No. 26
Sept. 7, 2008 • Richmond, Va. • Richmond International Raceway • 400 Laps

Jimmie Johnson and his Hendrick Motorsports team have had their share of ups and downs this season, but the two-time defending champion carried back-to-back wins into the 10-race playoff.

In the storm-delayed Chevy Rock & Roll 400 at Richmond International Raceway, Johnson put together a near-perfect race. He stayed close to the leaders, watched his crew push through a speedy pit stop and then nosed his way to the lead in the final laps. Johnson led the last 32 laps and held off a hungry-for-a-win Tony Stewart for the victory. Denny Hamlin, Dale Earnhardt Jr. and Mark Martin rounded out the top five.

"Fortunately [Jeff] Burton and I raced our butts off for about 50 laps earlier in the race, and I guess I learned a lesson through that whole thing," Johnson said.

For a driver and team that have lagged a bit behind Kyle Busch and Carl Edwards, this kind of rally has "championship contender" written all over it.

Johnson's fuel-mileage win at Phoenix earlier this season brought a sense of relief to the No. 48 team. His victory at Indianapolis was a sign of the team's continued strength, but it was marred by the notorious tire issues. The win at California proved his team could be dominant and sparked talk of a

three-man Chase showdown between Johnson, Busch and Edwards.

The triumph at Richmond? That moved him, in the minds of many, into the role of Chase favorite.

It certainly proved that a third straight championship was a real possibility and that the No. 48 team's emphasis on testing throughout the season is netting results.

"It is going well," crew chief Chad Knaus said. "We have been working all year for the championship. Jimmie is really doing a good job."

Aside from Johnson's entertaining and ultimately victorious side-by-side battle with Stewart, Earnhardt sent the crowd into a frenzy when he unintentionally spun Kyle Busch.

And, of course, there was the Chase.

Thanks to Tropical Storm Hanna washing out qualifying, the three drivers on the bubble — Clint Bowyer, David Ragan and Kasey Kahne — started 12th, 13th and 14th.

Soon after the race began, however, it became clear that Kahne didn't have a strong car. He couldn't get his No. 9 Dodge down to the bottom of the track and finished 19th. But the Gillett Evernham driver moved up to 13th in the standings — showing just how much Ragan struggled.

Ragan and his No. 6 team entered the cutoff race with high hopes. And the way he began, there was no reason to think he wouldn't contend for another top-five. Through the first 120 laps, Ragan was running seventh and sat just 25 points behind Bowyer.

But on lap 122 of 400, he got loose, spun and banged the wall.

Ragan's car sustained damage but not enough to knock him out of the race. Still, the car wasn't handling properly and Ragan slipped backward. Then, Bowyer made contact with Regan Smith, sending him into Ragan, who hit the wall again.

If the Chase wasn't sealed before that, it was

then. Ragan never recovered and finished 32nd.

"Running 32nd, you don't deserve to make the Chase," he said. "Certainly, this race doesn't [reflect] how our season's gone. Regardless of how we ended up today, whether we made the Chase or not, it wasn't going to be solely on the Richmond race."

The final spot went to Bowyer, and he'll challenge Matt Kenseth, Stewart, Jeff Gordon, Kevin Harvick, Greg Biffle and Hamlin, all of whom secured Chase berths at Richmond, in addition to Busch, Earnhardt, Johnson, Edwards and Burton, who had all previously locked up their spots.

"Just making the Chase is a big deal," Bowyer said. "You know, with some momentum, I think we can do just fine."

—Red White

NOT SO FAST

Johnson Counters Edwards' Attack

Camping World RV 400 • NASCAR Sprint Cup Race No. 29
Sept. 28, 2008 • Kansas City, Kan. • Kansas Speedway • 267 Laps

Jimmie Johnson solidified his status as a contender for a third straight Sprint Cup championship by winning the Camping World RV 400 at Kansas Speedway.

The win vaulted Johnson to the top of the point standings, the first time the two-time defending champion has been in the lead this season.

Since Johnson's first full season in 2002, he's gone only one season (2003) without leading the points on at least one occasion. And the first time he led the point standings, during his rookie campaign, came after a 10th-place finish at Kansas Speedway.

"I think this was probably one of the best examples of a total team effort — from Jimmie just driving the wheels off the car, Chad [Knaus, crew chief] making the right adjustments when we were a little off, and the pit crew getting Jimmie out when they needed to," team owner Rick Hendrick said.

"I think this just kind of shows why they're champions, and I'm really proud of them because it was a hard-fought deal today."

Johnson's No. 48 Chevrolet was on autopilot for much of the day, starting from the pole and leading five times for 124 of 267 laps. His fifth win of the season, and 38th of his career, seemed well in hand.

Carl Edwards, though, had other ideas.

Heading down the backstretch on the final lap, Edwards leaned on his dirt-track racing background — driving into the turn deeper than he should have, hoping he had enough car control to keep his red rocket off the wall.

He streaked by Johnson and into the lead, but Johnson wasn't worried.

"I knew instantly that there was no damn way he's making the turn," Johnson said. "I just stayed on the brake, tried to get redirected and turned down."

Carrying too much speed, Edwards' car drifted up the track and smacked the wall.

"I was in awe of how fast he drove it in," Johnson said. "I watched him pound the wall and jump back on the gas. I thought, 'Man, he's serious

about this win, I better get back on the gas myself.'"

Johnson may have underestimated how badly Edwards wanted the win, but Edwards clearly misjudged how hard he drove into the corner.

"That last lap, I just figured the hell with it," Edwards said. "I don't want to finish second here; I want to win this race more than anything in the world. So I kind of banzai-ed it in there.

"I planned on hitting the wall, but I didn't plan on the wall slowing me down that much."

Edwards recovered to finish second, and Greg Biffle, winner of the first two Chase races, finished third.

Chase drivers took the top seven spots, but it was far from an easy day for the majority of them.

Jeff Gordon finished fourth despite a case of the flu that kept him in his motorcoach for most of the weekend.

Matt Kenseth, Kevin Harvick and Jeff Burton were fifth through seventh. Burton rallied from the back of the field after a tachometer problem kept him on pit road prior to the start of the race.

Denny Hamlin, Clint Bowyer and Dale Earnhardt Jr. fashioned top-15 runs.

It wasn't as good a day for the remaining Chase drivers. Kyle Busch battled fuel-pressure problems before finishing 28th. Joe Gibbs Racing teammate Tony Stewart had problems in the pits and on the track en route to his 40th-place finish.

—Kenny Bruce

SEIZING CONTROL

Johnson Extends Chase with Dominant Win

Tums QuikPak 500 • NASCAR Sprint Cup Race No. 32
Oct. 19, 2008 • Martinsville, Va. • Martinsville Speedway • 504 Laps

Don't let the green-white-checkered finish fool you. A two-lap overtime dash for the checkered flag added a dash of drama but it couldn't hide the fact that Jimmie Johnson dominated the Tums QuikPak 500 at Martinsville Speedway.

Starting from the pole after qualifying was rained out, the No. 48 led seven times for 339 of 504 laps, never dropped out of the top 15 and basically crushed all comers.

Johnson's win came so easily that after the race, he was already chomping at the bit for the next event.

"I'm ready to go to Atlanta," he said. "I wish we were dropping the green flag at Atlanta right now. ... I'm focused and want this so bad and am ready to get to it."

Johnson's victory extended his lead in the Chase standings to 149 points, up 80 points from the week before. He also became the official favorite to take the 2008 Cup and claim a place in history next to Cale Yarborough, the only other driver to win three straight titles.

But — at least for now — Johnson didn't want to worry about history.

"It's still not time," he said. "As long as I can hold off and just worry about winning races ... hopefully I can do that the next two or three races and then cruise on from there."

Although it might feel like déjà vu with the No. 48 out front once again in October, Johnson was careful to point out that the team had not started the season in championship form.

"We got off to a start we were not accustomed to, and that was frustrating," he said. "But it made our team stronger, made the relationships stronger inside the team and makes me really proud today to

be where we are — knowing that we flat-out sucked at the start of the season."

He might have been exaggerating — his team hasn't been out of the top 10 since the sixth race of the season, but by running away from second-place Dale Earnhardt Jr. and third-place Carl Edwards in a not-so-frantic finish, Johnson showed that he and his team were ready for the final push to Homestead.

Of course, not everyone was willing to concede the title to Johnson.

"He could have any sort of trouble the next two races and be right back there with us," said Edwards, who stayed at fourth in the championship points. "This isn't over until the last lap at Homestead, that's for sure."

While Johnson surged, Jeff Burton, the winner a week before, slipped from second to third in the standings due to a late-race pit-road penalty.

With 40 laps left, the No. 31 got caught in pit road traffic when fourth-place finisher Jeff Gordon pulled in front of him. Consequently, Burton entered his pit box at a severe angle, drifting across the pit boundary. After an already-slow pit stop, NASCAR penalized Burton and he slipped to 17th.

"We didn't know we were over the line until we already had the tires off," he said. "We needed to run a little bit better than we did today but we had a bad break there and we will move on."

Greg Biffle, meanwhile, capitalized on a 12th-place finish to move into second in the Chase, just three points ahead of Burton.

"I'm excited," Biffle said. "I can't wait [to get to the 1.5-mile tracks]. Hang on, we're gonna let it rip."

—Jay Pfeifer

HEAVY HITTER
Johnson Delivers Knockout Punch

Checker O'Reilly Auto Parts 500 • NASCAR Sprint Cup Race No. 35
Nov. 9, 2008 • Phoenix, Ariz. • Phoenix International Raceway • 313 Laps

Jimmie Johnson all but sealed up a third straight Sprint Cup title by driving to a convincing win in the Checker O'Reilly Auto Parts 500 at Phoenix International Raceway.

Johnson led 217 of 313 laps en route to the win over Kurt Busch, Jamie McMurray, Carl Edwards and Denny Hamlin.

Johnson stared down a host of unusual obstacles in the desert — including an unlikely rain shower that forced a 23-minute delay, and a dust storm. The wind, which blew constantly down the backstretch, slapped sand in the drivers' faces as they fought the sun barreling down the frontstretch.

Then, a nine-car wreck erupted with 40 laps to go and Scott Speed's car slammed into the rear of David Gilliland. The No. 38 came to rest on top of Speed's car, causing the day's second red flag as cleanup crews worked to unravel them.

Eventually, frogs and locusts probably would have fallen from the sky. The day was that unusual.

Cautions begat cautions. There were 10 in all, and that didn't include a post-checkered crash that crunched several cars.

Four cautions were called for debris. But, in the broader sense, "debris" was everyone in the field except Johnson, who won for the seventh time this

year and the 40th time in his career.

Most symbolic of Johnson's dominance on this particular Sunday, was a single run in the minutes following a midrace caution. He had led 102 straight laps and built a 4.7-second lead when debris caused the day's fifth caution. He lost the lead in the pits and started the ensuing green-flag run behind new leader McMurray. He hardly trailed long enough to read the print on the rear of the No. 26 before he went on to lead the final 95 laps.

Johnson said his Chevrolet was at its best when he shot past McMurray only seconds into the green-flag run.

"I didn't think I'd have an opportunity that soon, but as we went into [Turn 1] my car stuck and rotated, and I was dead back in the gas," Johnson said. "I took that opportunity to get by him. The car was just hooked up, and off we went."

After that surge, it was clear that Johnson, who won for the third straight time at Phoenix, could do basically whatever he wanted, go wherever he

wanted and mash whomever he wanted. It was just a matter of moving through the evening's many cautions. By day's end, he was the only driver to run all 313 laps in the top 15 and in fact, he was seldom out of the top two.

Entering the season finale at Homestead, Johnson was working on one of the most remarkable closing streaks in the sport's history. Since late August, when he was third in points, he had won five races and finished second in two others.

He took to the Florida oval with a 141-point advantage over Edwards, his nearest rival.

"I really think where we are in points is going to allow me to go to Homestead and take a little pressure off my brain," Johnson said. "We don't need to do anything stupid. At the same time, how cool would it be to win out? I'd love to do that."

Edwards, meanwhile, was disappointed with his fourth-place finish. He had to hope for the worst for Johnson, who needed only to finish 36th to clinch the championship.

"It's possible, not real probable, but I guarantee that isn't going to change the way we do business," Edwards said. "We're going to go to Homestead with everything we've got and be aggressive and try to win the race."

—Mike Hembree

MR. NICE GUY

Three-time Champion Jimmie Johnson Proves that Nice Guys Don't Always Finish Last

If you're hoping to read an exposé here on the REAL JIMMIE JOHNSON, a story on all of the Sprint Cup champion's unseen warts, you're out of luck.

Want to hear about how his competitors secretly dislike Johnson? Sorry.

Or about how, once the cameras go off, the mild-mannered Johnson turns rude? Our apologies.

Or maybe about how his image is an elaborate cover-up to keep his true personality from the public? Go fish.

Move along, folks. Nothing to see here.

The truth about Johnson is this: He's respectful, considerate, patient and friendly.

To his fellow competitors. To his team. To fans. Even to the media.

The guy who has now won three Cup championships in a row just so happens to be one of the nicest guys around.

"Nice guys can finish first," two-time Cup champion Ned Jarrett said. "Our sport is in good hands when you see guys ... like Jimmie Johnson that are the leaders of it now. It's better to me to see the nice guys winning and fighting for championships."

Not everyone would agree. These days, it seems everyone is anxious for controversy. Fans wonder why someone doesn't just take Johnson out.

There's just one problem with that: Johnson is almost universally liked in the garage. He has the respect of his competitors, from fellow drivers to crew chiefs to crew members.

If they could loathe him, they would. But they can't.

"Sometimes I wish I could hate him a little more, make it more fun. But I just think he's a good guy," said his closest rival this year, Carl Edwards.

In today's sports world, the athletes who often get the most attention are the ones performing over-the-top celebrations, making controversial comments and generally hogging the spotlight. For them, life is about me, me, me; not team, team, team.

Johnson goes against all that. His values and beliefs guide him down a path of respect for his fellow competitors and the sport.

"I don't know why we have to be a circus act to make it a good show. Good competition and respect for one another should be plenty," Johnson said.

Nothing To Hide

Johnson spoke those words three days before winning his third consecutive title, part of a news conference that previewed the season finale and honored some of NASCAR's all-time great champions.

In the front row of the audience sat legends such as Richard Petty, Darrell Waltrip and Bobby Allison. As reporters quizzed Johnson and Edwards on the lack of a rivalry and the absence of hostility between the drivers, the past champions listened to Johnson's comments and silently nodded their approval.

The very nature of racing would seem to require its competitors be hard-nosed, on the edge, aggressive and perhaps somewhat of a jerk. It seems that nice guys would have a hard time thriving in a sport that requires its athletes to drive as hard as possible.

Perhaps that's why Johnson doesn't get as much attention – or as much credit, at times – as drivers such as Tony Stewart and Kyle Busch. He's calm, cool and polite, not the kind of driver you notice until he's standing in victory lane.

All About Respect

There's nothing about a driver's popularity that makes his car go faster. Other drivers aren't going to move out of the way just because a more famous competitor is in the rearview mirror.

But they will move out of the way – or at least not race someone as hard – if they've been treated with respect in the past. And Johnson has nearly perfected that element of his racing.

If Johnson doesn't have the best car, he won't hold up a faster driver. And in NASCAR, most drivers race one another on a case-by-case basis.

Race me hard, I'll race you hard. Cut me some slack, I'll remember that down the road.

When coming upon lapped cars in a championship Chase, that can make a major difference.

After a recent Chase race, Johnson cited Juan Pablo Montoya, Jamie McMurray and Stewart as drivers who worked with him that day.

"Guys that I'm catching them, slowly, but surely chipping away at it, they just pulled over and let me go. I have done that for them in the past," Johnson said. "Each situation is different, and it's nice to have friends out there that will work with you instead of guys taking shots at you all the time."

Just Good People

When Johnson came up through the ranks, there were countless people along the way who helped him, offered advice and shared information. Part of his philosophy now is to do the same for others, even if it someday costs him on the track.

"If somebody has a question, I'll answer truthfully," he said. "I'll help out, because that's helped

me get to where I am today."

Edwards, who tirelessly chased Johnson over the final weeks of the season in an effort to overtake him in the standings, acknowledges that "if I needed some advice or some help or something like that, I could go over to Jimmie and he'd be right there helping me out."

And that's a good feeling.

"It's more fun to race with folks like that, that you don't necessarily harbor any ill will toward," Edwards said.

In Johnson's mind, getting along with people in the garage and having friendships is of the utmost importance, and that means going out of his way to be nice when he doesn't have to.

It's hard for other drivers to dislike a guy like that.

"To this day when we have a good run, Jimmie is one of the first people to come over and congratulate me," Edwards said. "And when he has a good run, as much as it hurts us in the points sometimes, it's still good to see good people succeed."

—Jeff Gluck

MAKING HISTORY 2008

SILVER AND GOLD

Hendrick Celebrates 25th Anniversary with a Win

Goody's Fast Pain Relief 500 • NASCAR Sprint Cup Race No. 6
March 29, 2009 • Martinsville, Va. • Martinsville Speedway • 500 Laps

Hendrick Motorsports has experienced highs and lows at Martinsville Speedway. Since 1984, when Geoffrey Bodine delivered the team's first victory at the Virginia short track (and first in Cup competition), HMS has won 18 races at Martinsville, including nine of the last 12.

Jimmie Johnson has won six of those races —

including the October 2004 event just hours after a Hendrick plane crashed near Martinsville, killing four members of Rick Hendrick's family as well as six others — and this year's Goody's Fast Pain Relief 500.

Running second to Denny Hamlin with 16 laps to go, Johnson nudged Hamlin out of the groove and went on to take the win—his first of the 2009 season.

"People assume and expect us to win [here]," Johnson said. "We don't take this for granted. At the end, when I was trying to get back by Denny, it was in my mind that it would be awfully special to win for Rick here and win the 25th anniversary of his first win."

Hendrick credits crew chief Chad Knaus for much of Johnson's success at Martinsville. That's appropriate, considering that he believes that first victory came thanks to the knowledge of crew chief Harry Hyde.

"It's nothing about me," Hendrick said. "You know, I have very little to do with it. It's the organization. I think Harry Hyde started it. He loved this place."

Johnson, the three-time defending Cup champion, did not dominate the race like he has before. Teammate Jeff Gordon paced the field for 141 of the first 155 laps.

While Gordon was leading and cruising, Johnson's team was working on his car. A long pit stop for adjustments put him as far back as 25th at the 100-lap mark.

Johnson gradually improved, passing Hamlin for the lead on lap 430. He lost the top spot on lap 456 after Hamlin blew by him on a restart, but muscled his way back in front.

"We're very relieved to get the first one of the season," Johnson said. "I think it's a huge confidence booster for the new guys that are on our race team. It's a confidence booster for Chad and I. We didn't have an easy day today.

"We had to stay together as a team, work through a lot of changes, a loss of track position to make the car better and fight for the front, count on

pit stops, count on good driving."

Hamlin, who led 296 laps, believed Johnson intentionally pushed him aside, while Johnson argued that Hamlin chopped down on him.

"Denny, if he wants to think that I tried moving him out of the way, he can believe that," Johnson said. "But he should watch the video; I was inside of him. I did everything I could to miss him. I climbed up on the curb, and [he was] still coming down. The only reason we touched, the only reason he ended up in the rubber — where he couldn't come back and get me — was the fact that he chopped."

Whether Johnson shoved him aside or not, Hamlin shouldn't have been surprised to see Johnson in victory lane again. After all, this is a Hendrick track.

—**Bob Pockrass**

CUTTING IT CLOSE

Johnson's Late-Race Surge Secures Win

Autism Speaks 400 • NASCAR Sprint Cup Race No. 13
May 31, 2009 • Dover, Del. • Dover International Speedway • 400 Laps

Jimmie Johnson steamrolled the competition in the Autism Speaks 400 at Dover International Speedway.

Johnson led chunks of 67, 35, 67, 36, 47 and 32 laps at Dover by margins of several seconds before caution flags bunched the field.

"We've been fast, but this was a very special race car today," Johnson said.

Johnson's day was nearly ruined, however, during the final round of pit stops. The crew of the No. 48 Hendrick Motorsports Chevrolet struggled while changing the left front tire, and the three-time series champion took the race's final green flag in eighth place with just 27 laps to go.

"Unfortunately, we had a little hiccup on the last stop," crew chief Chad Knaus said. "We came out eighth and really had to lean on Jimmie a little to carry us out. He did a great job."

Contributing to Johnson's drop from first to eighth during the pit stop round was the fact that some drivers — including frontrunners Greg Biffle and Tony Stewart — chose to change only two tires to gain track position.

Johnson was forced to push his car to the limit, but he was up to third behind leader Biffle and Stewart by lap 380 of 400.

With nine laps to go, Stewart rolled into first and Johnson followed him into second.

The two drivers played a cat-and-mouse game in the final five laps — Johnson moving out of the lower groove to find cleaner air and less traffic up high, and Stewart moving in both directions trying

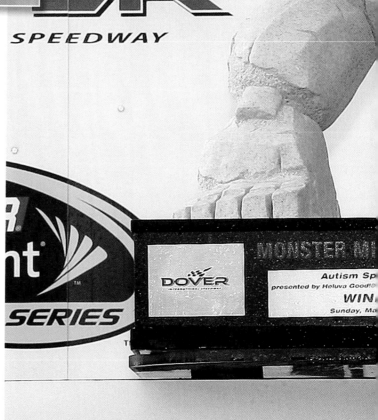

to deny Johnson passing room.

Johnson made several runs at Stewart before getting around him in Turn 3.

"To have to run that hard and pass that many good cars to get the lead, that's a challenge," Johnson said. "I thought I was going to pound the wall a couple of times.

"I got up there in third and started hunting those guys down. My hat's off to Tony Stewart. That was one heck of a race. I had to drive so far over my head to get by him."

Stewart held on to finish second and Biffle, Matt Kenseth and Kurt Busch rounded out the top five.

Although he didn't win the race, the day was a significant one for Stewart. He jumped from second into the points lead — thus becoming the first owner/driver to lead the standings since Alan Kulwicki at the end of the 1992 season.

"When you're the fastest car and you're coming as fast as [Johnson] was, it was just a matter of getting the opening that he needed, and we did everything we could to take his line away from him as often as we could," Stewart said. "But I just couldn't do it long enough."

—Mike Hembree

TWICE IS NICE

Johnson Wins Second Straight, Third of Career at Indy

Allstate 400 at The Brickyard • NASCAR Sprint Cup Race No. 20
July 26, 2009 • Indianapolis, Ind. • Indianapolis Motor Speedway • 160 Laps

Thanks to a critical error by Juan Pablo Montoya, Jimmie Johnson ran away with his second straight win at Indianapolis Motor Speedway.

Starting second, Montoya grabbed the lead on lap five and with a few exceptions, led until lap 125.

"I was cruising," Montoya said. "The car was stupid fast."

But it wouldn't last. On a green-flag pit stop, NASCAR tagged Montoya with a pass-through penalty for speeding.

The apoplectic Montoya couldn't believe that he had been speeding, saying over his team radio, "I swear on my children and my wife I wasn't speeding."

The penalty dropped him from first to 12th and, without clean air, he struggled to move through traffic on his way to an 11th-place finish.

After the race, Montoya had cooled down, accepting the penalty without necessarily agreeing with it.

"It is what it is. I thought I was on the speed," he said. "We have lights. I was on the lights every time. I was where I was on the previous one and they say I was speeding."

Almost immediately after Montoya served his penalty, the engine in Dale Earnhardt Jr.'s No. 88 blew up and spilled oil near the entry of pit road, bringing out the third and final caution of the day and opening the door for Johnson.

Johnson started the race 16th but rocketed into the top five by lap 30. However his progress slowed and the last yellow flag finally gave him a chance to grab the lead.

"It was just very tough to come through the field," Johnson said. "We started 16th. Kind of fell

into fifth for a while, got to fourth, then to third. At the end with Juan having his problems, the caution coming out, it gave me a chance to really race with Mark [Martin] on the restart. That was really my only opportunity."

Johnson didn't waste his chance. On the final restart with 24 laps to go, the three-time Cup champion roared past Martin and managed to keep the No. 5 behind him the rest of the way.

Though Martin nipped at Johnson's heels, he could never quite pass him.

"I absolutely could not go any faster," Martin said. "In fact, I can't believe I didn't. The third-to-last lap and the last lap, I went through there beyond my good judgment to get those runs. It just wasn't enough."

"I did everything I could on that restart," Johnson said. "It worked out. I cleared him. At the end he was coming a little bit on me. Got a little

loose in Turns 1 and 2, but the car was really good in Turns 3 and 4. We were kind of trading off the distance."

Despite an enviable record that includes three wins this season, Johnson is still haunted by a couple wins he and his team have left on the table.

"We've been very fast and have led a lot of laps the last couple months, but we haven't been able to be in the right spot at the end. It's been a little frustrating," Johnson said. "So to have it all come full circle today, lead at the right time, win this thing, meant a lot to us."

Tony Stewart finished behind Martin to claim his 12th top-10 of 2009. Greg Biffle and Brian Vickers rounded out the top five.

—Jay Pfeifer

LOUD AND CLEAR

Johnson Sends Message with Dover Win

AAA 400 • NASCAR Sprint Cup Race No. 28
Sept. 27, 2009 • Dover, Del. • Dover International Speedway • 400 Laps

The mood in the Sprint Cup garage was glum after Jimmie Johnson drove to victory in the AAA 400 at Dover International Speedway.

Ryan Newman strode briskly toward the exit and dismissed an interview request with a wave of his hand. Eyes red, Greg Biffle offered just one sentence and walked away. Denny Hamlin looked as though someone had just run over his dog.

"Yeah. Makes you feel a little sick," said Carl Edwards, who finished 11th. "I didn't realize he won until he was out there doing burnouts. You know, they earn it. They're good. They work hard."

With the win, Johnson, crew chief Chad Knaus and the No. 48 Hendrick Motorsports team showed they're serious about nailing down a fourth straight championship. Johnson is just that good, and perhaps no one outside of Mark Martin, who finished second at Dover, is capable of stopping him.

Biffle was asked how bad it was for everyone else that Johnson dominated the race (he led a race-high 271 laps to complete a season sweep) at Dover.

"How bad is it for the competition to see the 48 tire test in the Chase?" Biffle shot back. "That's all I'm going to say."

Biffle was referring to the Goodyear tire test in August, where Johnson was invited along with sev-

eral others to help the manufacturer select a proper tire for the race. Some of the drivers grumbled about Johnson getting an unfair advantage.

Of course, as Johnson pointed out twice during the Dover weekend, he never complained about not being able to test at Indianapolis Motor Speedway even though many other competitors had tested at the 2.5-mile track. And Johnson went on to win the Brickyard without that advantage.

"There are some guys that can't help but say

stuff time after time," Johnson said, shrugging off Biffle's comments.

But in some ways, Johnson didn't exactly mind that his win was causing such a flood of bad feelings in the garage.

"As far as sending a message, I hope it does," he said. "I hope people talk about it. I hope people are worried. I hope people are talking about the fact that we tire tested and it's wrong. All these people can get wound up about stuff that really doesn't matter."

It was hard to imagine that Johnson's Dover domination didn't send a message. Even the double-file restarts, which have improved racing so dramatically this season, were no match for Johnson. No matter who lined up beside him, he simply pulled away.

Johnson had everyone covered — though non-Chaser Matt Kenseth managed a third-place finish, his first top-five since the last Dover race in May. But that was about it, as Johnson led each of the final 224 laps of the 400-lap race.

"Maximum points!" he said on the team radio. "Thank you!"

In winning three straight championships, Johnson has refused to play mind games after an attempt to do so with Tony Stewart in 2005 failed. Instead, he said, he "puts the blinders on" and doesn't follow the news to find out what people are saying about his chances.

But the idea of letting his dominant win speak for itself sounded like something Johnson could support.

"I certainly hope that our performance today scares some people and affects them in a way that benefits us," he said.

As if he needed any more help.

—Jeff Gluck

POINT MAN
Win Puts Johnson Out Front

Pepsi 500 • NASCAR Sprint Cup Race No. 30
Oct. 11, 2009 • Fontana, Calif. • Auto Club Speedway • 250 Laps

Jimmie Johnson dominated the Pepsi 500 at Auto Club Speedway like a Sprint Cup champion should. You could almost say that Johnson once again served notice that this is his championship to lose — just as it was in 2008, 2007 and 2006.

While Johnson left his competition in the dust, the drivers in his rearview mirror were the same as those tailing him in the point standings.

Hendrick Motorsports teammate Jeff Gordon, fifth in points, finished second. Juan Pablo Montoya, third in points, finished third, Mark Martin, the former points leader who slipped to second, finished fourth, and Tony Stewart rebounded from a speeding penalty to finish fifth and remain fourth in the standings.

It might be Johnson's title to lose, but there's plenty of stiff competition to snatch it if he falters.

"We're in a great position, but it's way too early to start thinking about [the title]," Johnson said. "We love the fact that we're in the points lead. We got maximum points today. But I don't want to go there."

If Johnson isn't thinking about locking up a fourth title, his competition is thinking about what it will take to catch him.

Montoya probably had the second-best car in California, but Johnson's car improved as the

cloud cover lifted during the race, he led 104 of the final 126 laps.

"We have four [top-fives] in a row and I've been losing points to the leader," Montoya said. "You ain't going to make any points on anybody. Everybody that runs good is going to be there. You just got to make sure you don't lose any."

If it wasn't for Montoya, it could be an all-Hendrick Chase with Johnson, Martin and Gordon. Throw Stewart in there as well considering his team has a technical alliance with Hendrick.

Even though he lost the points lead, Martin was grinning from ear to ear. Was it exciting that three Hendrick cars finished in the top four or deflating considering those three are among his

main competitors for the title?

"Neither," Martin said. "It's just racing. We all race when we're on the track, and I'm not thinking about it off the track. It was just a really incredible job."

Finishing fourth and losing the lead in the championship showed just how tight the points race is. It made every move critical, especially considering there were three restarts in the final 12 laps.

Johnson didn't get a good push on the restart with 12 laps remaining and Gordon bolted by him. He held on for five laps before another restart and Johnson whizzed by him to take the lead for good.

"The only thing to me that's bittersweet is that we finished second, and I felt like we were in a second-class category," Gordon said. "That's the only

thing that bothers me a little bit. We're just not good enough. We're good, but we're not good enough."

It seems that no matter how good anyone is in the 10 races that comprise NASCAR's playoffs, Johnson and crew chief Chad Knaus run up front.

Johnson credits the tracks, saying they are among the best for him of the 22 that make up the Sprint Cup circuit.

Maybe it's something else.

"They have something magical about the final 10 races," Gordon said. "You know, these 10 tracks really suit them. They do an incredible job. What else can you say? They're the best out there.

"They've won the last three championships. They're going to be hard to beat for this one. Really, unless they make a mistake, I don't see how they lose it."

—Bob Pockrass

THE UNTOUCHABLES

No. 48 Team Tightens Grip on Title

NASCAR Banking 500 only from Bank of America • NASCAR Sprint Cup Race No. 31
Oct. 17, 2009 • Concord, N.C. • Lowe's Motor Speedway • 334 Laps

No matter which way the question was asked, Jimmie Johnson, crew chief Chad Knaus and team owner Rick Hendrick all kept insisting the same thing: the Chase is not over.

But when questioned on whether Johnson is "stinking up the show" by winning three of the first five Chase races — including the NASCAR Banking 500 at Lowe's Motor Speedway — and holding a commanding lead halfway through NASCAR's play-offs, Johnson compared his situation to those of the most dominant athletes on the planet.

"I don't understand why people would have a problem with it," Johnson said. "Everybody tunes in to watch Tiger [Woods] win. Everybody tunes in to watch [Roger] Federer do his thing on certain courts. I'm just doing my thing."

At LMS, that included leading all three practices, winning the pole, leading the most laps and walking off with his sixth win of the season.

The most impressive thing about Johnson's latest run has been that despite the massive target on his back, no one can stop him.

Like a giant shrugging off boulder attacks as if they were pebbles, Johnson stood tall as the biggest threats to a 48 four-peat crumbled.

Juan Pablo Montoya had strung together a Cinderella run with four consecutive top-five finishes to begin the Chase. He had even outrun Johnson at times, an accomplishment which may someday result in a NASCAR trophy.

Yet Montoya found trouble on several restarts, and the resulting contact damaged his car. He finished a disappointing 35th — four laps down — and

dropped from third to sixth in the standings.

"Oh, it's OK," Montoya said. "It's racing. If you're expecting to have 10 clean races, then you're dreaming."

But somehow, that dream continues for Johnson. The driver of the No. 48 car has now gone an incredible 31 straight races in the Chase without finishing outside the top 15.

Johnson is so good, he out-runs the bad luck and misfortune that plagues other drivers.

Take Carl Edwards, for example. He flopped to 10th in the Chase after finishing 39th at Charlotte.

"That's the most frustrated I've been in a long time, but you can't do anything about it," he said. "This is auto racing; a thousand things have to go right, and if any of them go wrong, your night is bad."

Another former contender, Denny Hamlin, declared his title chances finished after he, like Edwards, blew a motor and finished 42nd. Prior to the Chase, he had declared himself as the best hope to knock off Johnson.

"We're definitely done as far as the championship is concerned," Hamlin said. "The way that we're running, we belong up top. A couple of mistakes take you right out of it.

"If you have one bad week, whether because of a driver mistake or a parts failure, you're done. Your season's over. That part of it is frustrating."

Even Mark Martin, who looked as if he'd be able to make a run for the title, lost ground to Johnson at Charlotte.

The 50-year-old has always called Charlotte one of his favorite tracks, but he finished a disappointing 17th — which widened the gap to Johnson from 12 to 90 points.

"I don't know where we missed it," Martin said. "I don't know what we did wrong. It was just a tough night for us. It was just one of those nights where everything wasn't right on.

"You're going to have days like this."

Not Johnson. The 34-year-old Californian tied Buck Baker for 13th on NASCAR's all-time win list with 46 and moved into a tie with Darrell Waltrip and Bobby Allison for the most all-time victories at Charlotte (six), the home track for most NASCAR teams.

Johnson's stellar run might not sit well with everyone, but the Hendrick driver isn't offering any apologies.

"I think there are a lot of fans out there excited to see what this 48 car is doing, and a lot of people are happy and rooting for us to win a fourth," he said. "The rest of them, oh well."

—Jeff Gluck

ALMOST THERE

Johnson Closes in on Title

Checker O'Reilly Auto Parts 500 Presented by Pennzoil • NASCAR Sprint Cup Race No. 35
Nov. 15, 2009 • Phoenix, Ariz. • Phoenix International Raceway • 312 Laps

Jimmie Johnson knocked out the competition and moved a step closer to securing his fourth straight Sprint Cup title by driving to victory in the Checker O'Reilly Auto Parts 500 at Phoenix International Raceway.

It was Johnson's seventh win of the season and fourth in the last five races at the 1-mile desert oval.

"We just put a butt-kicking on everybody today," said Johnson, who led 238 of 312 laps.

It was a familiar scene after the race: Johnson and the No. 48 team celebrating in victory lane while everyone else licked their wounds.

"I'm very proud of the fact we looked each other in the eyes, knew what we had to do and delivered," Johnson said. "It wasn't easy. You know, there was a lot of pressure on us to do this. All week long, thinking about this race, wondering if we could come back and step up like we did today, there were just a lot of thoughts that go through the brain. I'm very proud of how we delivered and rose to the occasion."

Jeff Burton rallied from a 36th-place qualifying run to finish second at Phoenix and score his best finish of 2009.

The finish was Burton's third consecutive top-10 and third in as many starts with crew chief Todd Berrier calling the shots.

"I have a lot of faith in Todd," Burton said. "I think Todd has a lot of faith in me. We're very blunt, very up front, very honest. We just go to work. He's real good about reminding me about things I need to be reminded of. He's everything I thought he was and more."

Denny Hamlin finished third at Phoenix for the fourth time in his career. Thanks to fast pit work during a final cycle of green-flag stops, Hamlin

emerged from pit road right behind Johnson with 65 laps to go.

Hamlin gave up second to Burton with 29 laps to go and held on from there to net his 14th top-five and 19th top-10 of the season.

"We finished where we usually do at this race track," Hamlin said. "No matter what you throw in the car, I'm the best of the worst or the worst of the best, one of the two."

Mark Martin finished fourth and trailed Johnson by 108 points heading into the season finale at Homestead-Miami Speedway.

"I'm not worried about it," Martin said of his deficit. "We've talked about this a million times. We had a great race today. I'm proud of what we did."

Polesitter Martin Truex Jr. earned his first top-five finish of the season. It came a little later than he wanted, as it's been mostly a forgettable year for the Earnhardt Ganassi Racing driver who is headed to

Michael Waltrip Racing next year.

"It's huge to me because those guys are just like brothers to me," Truex said. "We're just like a family. I wanted it so bad all year. I've been trying all year. I think sometimes we try too hard and that's what gets us in trouble and causes problems.

"To keep digging all year after the year we've had and not give up and come out here and get a top-five, I'm just real proud of their efforts.

"We didn't have any problems in the pits. Nothing fell off the car. The tires held air. You know, all that good stuff. We just had a good race. Nothing bad happened and we didn't have any bad luck."

—**Jeff Gluck**

THE JIMMIE JOHNSON ERA

Hendrick Star Takes His Place in History Among NASCAR's Greatest Drivers

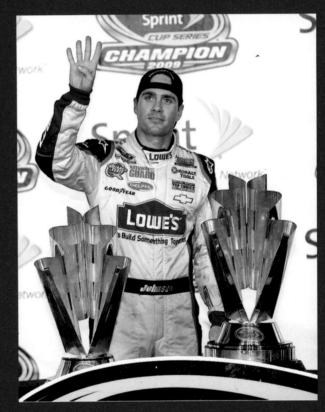

Decades from now, when Jimmie Johnson is no longer winning races and championships by the boatload, NASCAR historians will determine his place in the sport's history.

For now, let it be recorded that Johnson, who, at 34, might still be short of his peak, has reached a level of achievement not seen by the sport's other titans – racing royalty such as Richard Petty, Dale Earnhardt, Cale Yarborough, David Pearson, Darrell Waltrip, Bobby Allison and Jeff Gordon.

They put up impressive numbers, but they didn't do this: When Johnson sealed a fourth straight Sprint Cup championship at Homestead, he became the first driver in series history to rule the sport for four consecutive seasons.

The adjectives attempting to describe Johnson's achievement have flown forth from friend and foe: Incredible. Unbelievable. Fantastic. Remarkable.

Add to those: Mindnumbingly relentless.

"What he and that group have done – four in a row—is incredible," said former championship crew chief and team owner Ray Evernham, who won three titles in four years with Gordon. "It's an incredibly difficult feat in any sport because of the level of competition, the level of focus, the length of the season."

Think you might want to compete against Johnson and his Hendrick Motorsports guys? Think this trophy will be easy to pry from his icy fingers? Hope for a quick collapse of the 48 superstructure? Think again.

"Every time you come up with something you might want to do to your car ... Hendrick has already done it, and they're already on to something else," said former champion Rusty Wallace. "How in the hell do you have a fighting chance? If you dream up something, Hendrick has already been there."

The seal on the fourth championship was attached without a load of stress as Johnson finished fifth in the Ford 400, the season finale at Homestead-Miami Speedway. Although Johnson had a few touchy moments in heavy traffic early in the race, he was never in jeopardy of losing the title to the second-place driver, teammate Mark Martin. Martin finished 12th in the race and wound up 141 points behind Johnson in the final standings.

Johnson said he hopes to get a fifth straight title next year and ultimately to challenge the seven-championship standard set by Petty and Earnhardt.

He said the fourth straight title "has to put me up there [near the top of great driver lists]. The fact that nobody has done this, I think it puts me near

the top. And the cool thing is we're not done.

"What we've done is truly amazing. I don't know if we'll win another championship. There are no guarantees on that. I feel in my heart we'll be competitive. Yes, I would love to win seven or eight championships. Is it realistic with the level of competition we have? We're sure as hell going to try."

Regardless of what happens next year, for now, the Jimmie Johnson Era has officially continued. Petty never has been a fan of comparing drivers from different eras, but Johnson's run certainly has gotten his attention.

"There was an era that I kind of dominated," he said. "There was an era there that Earnhardt dominated. There was an era that Jeff Gordon dominated. This is Jimmie Johnson's era."

Martin, the primary victim of Johnson's fourth championship, said the true merit of what Johnson has accomplished won't be appreciated for some time.

"I think everyone has it tempered some," he said. "I don't think that they really realize that they're getting their brains beat in by that group like they really are in today's age. I think when we get 10, 20 years down the road and look back, people will realize what an incredible feat that they have achieved."

Johnson's success has been frustrating for the opposition.

"You go home some nights and think, 'Man, I should just get a job at the 7-Eleven,'" said Steve Hmiel, director of competition at Earnhardt Ganassi Racing. "What they've done is actually fantastic. They've taken pretty close to the same amount of horsepower [as everyone else], pretty close to the same amount of downforce, pretty close to the same amount of pit-stop times, the same systems, and they've whipped us."

The persistence of Johnson and the 48 team stands out in the views of competitors.

"Even when they're not that fast, they're just like that team that won't go away," Carl Edwards said. "They don't ever lay down. When they're not great, they're good. They're never bad. And that's what I think makes them so tough."

The idea that Johnson is a minor component in the overall Hendrick success – that virtually anyone could have driven the 48 cars to four straight titles – is rebuffed by series veterans.

"I listen to Jimmie over the radio," said Jimmy Makar, Joe Gibbs Racing senior vice president of racing operations. "I watch what he does on the race track. Jimmie Johnson is a student of the sport. He's looking at it and studying it all the time. You just listen to him and watch what he does. I think

he's different from a lot of people in that. He has impressed me in the way he's gone about trying to win races and get better over time."

Former Cup champion Dale Jarrett said he is amazed that Johnson's accomplishments haven't gained more respect and admiration.

"I don't think he gets the accolades he should," Jarrett said. "He works out extremely hard. He keeps himself in great physical condition. He thinks about this constantly. He's given up a lot to get to this point. I think the perception is because he has the best cars and the best team and the best crew chief in the business then why shouldn't he win? But we've seen other drivers with a lot of talent put in that position who couldn't get the job done. And he's done this not just for one year but four years."

And for a fifth? Stay tuned.

—Jeff Gluck

JJ WINS BY YEAR

2006

February 19, 2006
Daytona 500
Daytona International
Speedway
Daytona Beach, Florida
Started: 9
Laps Led: 24 of 203

March 12, 2006
UAW-DaimlerChrysler 400
Las Vegas Motor Speedway
Las Vegas, Nevada
Started: 3
Laps Led: 1 of 270

May 1, 2006
Aaron's 499
Talladega Superspeedway
Talladega, Alabama
Started: 16
Laps Led: 3 of 188

August 6, 2006
Allstate 400 at The Brickyard
Indianapolis Motor Speedway
Indianapolis, Indiana
Started: 5
Laps Led: 33 of 160

October 22, 2006
Subway 500
Martinsville Speedway
Martinsville, Virginia
Started: 9
Laps Led: 245 of 500

2007

March 11, 2007
UAW-DaimlerChrysler 400
Las Vegas Motor Speedway
Las Vegas, Nevada
Started: 23
Laps Led: 89 of 267

March 18, 2007
Kobalt Tools 500
Atlanta Motor Speedway
Hampton, Georgia
Started: 3
Laps Led: 135 of 325

April 1, 2007
Goody's Cool Orange 500
Martinsville Speedway
Martinsville, Virginia
Started: 20
Laps Led: 113 of 500

May 6, 2007
Crown Royal 400
Richmond International
Raceway
Richmond, Virginia
Started: 4
Laps Led: 105 of 400

September 2, 2007
Sharp Aquos 500
California Speedway
Fontana, California
Started: 3
Laps Led: 84 of 250

September 8, 2007
Chevy Rock & Roll 400
Richmond International
Raceway
Richmond, Virginia
Started: 1
Laps Led: 104 of 400

October 21, 2007
Subway 500
Martinsville Speedway
Martinsville, Virginia
Started: 4
Laps Led: 147 of 506

October 28, 2007
Pep Boys Auto 500
Atlanta Motor Speedway
Hampton, Georgia
Started: 6
Laps Led: 8 of 329

November 4, 2007
Dickies 500
Texas Motor Speedway
Fort Worth, Texas
Started: 8
Laps Led: 9 of 334

November 11, 2007
Checker Auto Parts 500
Phoenix International
Raceway
Phoenix, Arizona
Started: 6
Laps Led: 55 of 312

POWER PASSION PRIDE

How Jimmie Johnson and the No. 48 Team Made History

Triumph Books
542 South Dearborn Street
Suite 750
Chicago, Illinois 60605
(312) 939-3330
Fax (312) 663-3557
www.triumphbooks.com

All text and editorial provided by NASCAR Illustrated and NASCAR Scene

All photography by:
Sam Cranston
Jim Fluharty
David Griffin
Bambi Mattila
Patrick Schneider
Mark Sluder

Cover design by Valerie Helvey
Page design by Joe Funk and Jason Hinman

Printed in U.S.A.
ISBN: 978-1-60078-427-9